FRENCH GRAMMAR WORKBOOK

50 French Grammar and Conjugation Activities for Daily Practice

DYLANE MOREAU

TABLE OF CONTENTS

PREFACE

Welcome to the *French Grammar Workbook*, a comprehensive guide designed for high beginners to intermediate learners of French. This workbook offers a collection of 50 activities that cover the most common French grammar and conjugation rules, allowing you to deepen your understanding and mastery of the French language.

The activities in this workbook are made into bite-size lessons, allowing you to practice French daily even when you have little time for your learning journey.

Each chapter is dedicated to a specific grammar or conjugation rule, providing clear explanations and engaging exercises to help you learn, review, and practice confidently. Whether you're looking to solidify your foundation or refine your skills, this book offers a practical approach with easy-to-understand examples in French.

An answer key is provided at the end of the book to support your learning further, and free downloadable audio is available to improve your listening comprehension skills.

This workbook is perfect for daily practice. The *French Grammar Workbook* is part of a three-book series, including the *French Vocabulary Workbook* and the *French Listening Workbook*, which allows you to practice different aspects of French daily.

I hope this workbook will be a valuable companion on your journey to becoming more proficient in French. Happy learning!

Dylane

HOW TO USE THIS BOOK

If you want to refine your understanding of the most common French grammar and conjugation rules, this book is perfect for you. To maximize your learning experience, here are some helpful tips:

- Take advantage of the note pages throughout the book. Keep track of the vocabulary you learned, the questions you got right and the ones you got wrong. Come back to your notes often to review them.
- Pace Yourself: Instead of doing all the lessons and exercises in one sitting, try focusing on one chapter and one rule per day.
- Do the exercises: Each chapter ends with an exercise to practice what you just learned or reviewed. Since French and English grammar don't match, the examples used in the exercises are translated. I want you to understand the examples to get the right grammar in French.
- Improve Your Listening Skills: Take advantage of the free audio download and listen to each activity while simultaneously reading the text. This technique will help you connect spoken and written French and may improve your pronunciation.

By following these tips, you'll improve your French grammar and conjugation quickly!

Have fun learning!

HOW TO DOWNLOAD THE AUDIO

To download the audio files of all the recordings in this book, visit

www.theperfectfrench.com/french-grammar-workbook-audios

or scan the **QR code** below.

After entering your email, the link for the audio download will be sent directly to your inbox with step-by-step instructions. If you encounter an issue, please send me an email at **info@theperfectfrench.com**

UN – UNE – DES
A – SOME

1

Un, une, and des *(a)* are indefinite articles in French. They change depending on if the noun is masculine, feminine, singular, or plural. We use them to talk about **unspecific things** or **people**.

AUDIO 1.1 🔊

	Masculine	**Feminine**
Singular	**Un** – *A*	**Une** – *A*
	Un chien – *A dog*	**Une maison** – *A house*
Plural	**Des** – *Some/any*	**Des** – *Some/any*
	Des chiens – *Dogs*	**Des maisons** – *Houses*

French indefinite articles are quite easy and are used the same way as in English. All you need to know is the gender of the following noun.

J'ai <u>un</u> chien et <u>un</u> chat.
I have a dog and a cat.

AUDIO 1.2 🔊

 Ajoutez **un, une** ou **des** aux phrases suivantes.
Add un, une, or des to the following sentences.

1. Est-ce que tu veux _____ café ?
   Do you want a coffee?

2. Elle a _____ bonne idée pour ton cadeau d'anniversaire.
   She has a great idea for your birthday present.

3. Mes parents travaillent dans _____ magasin de décoration.
   My parents work in a home decor store.

4. C'est important d'avoir   chambre propre.

It's important to have a clean room.

5. On a planté   arbres pour avoir un peu d'ombre dans le jardin.

We planted trees to provide some shade in the garden.

6. Il y a   oranges sur la table.

There are oranges on the table.

7. Casser   miroir porte malheur.

Breaking a mirror brings bad luck.

8. C'est   idée géniale !

This is a brilliant idea!

9. Je pense qu'elle a   nouveau téléphone.

I think she has a new phone.

10. Il y a   croissants pour le petit déjeuner.

There are croissants for breakfast.

11. On a reçu   invitation mais ce n'est pas pour nous.

We received an invitation but it's not for us.

12. J'habite dans   petit appartement.

I live in a small apartment.

13. Cette voiture a   options intéressantes.

This car has some interesting options.

14. Il y a   personne dans la salle d'attente.

There is a person in the waiting room.

15. N'oublie pas de faire   vœu !

Don't forget to make a wish!

LE PLURIEL DES NOMS
PLURAL OF NOUNS

2

French nouns can be either singular or plural. A noun becomes plural when it represents more than one object, person, place, idea, etc. When plural, their endings change (besides one type of ending) but aren't always pronounced.

Make sure to listen to the audio to hear the difference or no difference in some cases.

Nouns ending in **-e** will simply take an **-s** when plural.

AUDIO 2.1 ◄))

Une plante – *A plant*   **Des plante<u>s</u>** – *Plants*

For nouns ending in **-s, -x** or **-z**, the ending doesn't change.

AUDIO 2.2 ◄))

Un bras – *An arm*   **Des bras** – *Arms*
Un prix – *A price*   **Des prix** – *Prices*
Un nez – *A nose*   **Des nez** – *Noses*

For nouns ending in **-eau**, **-au**, or **-eu**, the ending will simply take an **-x**.

AUDIO 2.3 ◄))

Un drapeau – *A flag*   **Des drapeau<u>x</u>** – *Flags*
Un noyau – *A pit*   **Des noyau<u>x</u>** – *Pits*
Un feu – *A fire*   **Des feu<u>x</u>** – *Fires*

Nouns ending in **-ou** take an **-s** but have quite a few exceptions that will take an **-x**.

AUDIO 2.4 ◄))

Un bisou – *A kiss*   **Des bisou<u>s</u>** – *Kisses*

Exceptions:

Des bijou<u>x</u> – *Jewelry* | **Des caillou<u>x</u>** – *Rocks* | **Des chou<u>x</u>** – *Cabbages*
Des genou<u>x</u> – *Knees* | **Des hibou<u>x</u>** – *Owls* | **Des joujou<u>x</u>** – *Toys* | **Des pou<u>x</u>** – *Lice*

Nouns ending in **-al** change into **-aux**; exceptions will only take an **-s**.

AUDIO 2.5 ◄))

Un total – *A total* **Des totaux** – *Totals*

Exceptions:

Des bals – *Balls* | **Des carnavals** – *Carnivals* | **Des festivals** – *Festivals*
Des récitals – *Recitals*

Nouns ending in **-ail** will only take an **-s**, but the exceptions will change for **-aux**.

AUDIO 2.6 ◄))

Un détail – *A detail* **Des détails** – *Details*

Exceptions:

Un bail - **Des baux** – *Leases* | **Un corail** - **Des coraux** – *Corals* | **Un émail** - **Des émaux** –
Enamels | **Un soupirail** - **Des soupiraux** – *Windows* | **Un travail** - **Des travaux** – *Works*
Un vitrail - **Des vitraux** – *Stained glasses*

Nouns ending in **a consonant** (besides -s and -x) will take an **-s** when plural.

AUDIO 2.7 ◄))

Un rat – *A rat* **Des rats** – *Rats*
Un nid – *A nest* **Des nids** – *Nests*

Some nouns have an irregular plural. Here are four of the most common ones.

AUDIO 2.8 ◄))

Monsieur – *Sir* **Messieurs** – *Sirs*
Madame – *Ma'am* **Mesdames** – *Ma'ams*
Mademoiselle – *Miss* **Mesdemoiselles** – *Misses*
Un œil – *An eye* **Des yeux** – *Eyes*

AUDIO 2.9 ◄))

 Transformez ces noms du **singulier** au **pluriel**.
Change these nouns from singular to plural.

1. On va jouer à des _____ **(jeu)** de société ce soir.
    We're going to play board games tonight.

2. La laine est pleine de _____ **(nœud)**.
    The yarn is full of knots.

3. Certains **(animal)** sont en danger d'extinction.

Some animals are in danger of extinction.

4. J'ai deux **(chien)** et deux **(chat)**.

I have two dogs and two cats.

5. Les **(oiseau)** attendent que je lance des **(graine)**.

The birds are waiting for me to throw seeds.

6. Je ne trouve pas les **(clou)** pour réparer le plancher.

I can't find the nails to fix the floor.

7. Il y a trop de **(choix)**.

There are too many choices.

8. Ces **(client)** ont réservé la salle numéro 3.

These clients have reserved room number 3.

9. J'aime écouter des **(chanson)** quand je travaille.

I like to listen to songs when I work.

10. Ça fait toujours plaisir de recevoir des **(fleur)**.

It's always nice to receive flowers.

11. Les **(repas)** sont servis à dix-neuf heures.

Meals are served at 7 p.m.

12. Il a perdu beaucoup de **(cheveu)**.

He lost a lot of hair.

13. On utilise des **(journal)** pour commencer le feu.

We use newspapers to start the fire.

14. Les **(bocal)** ne sont pas propres.

The jars are not clean.

15. Est-ce que tu as lu ces **(roman)** ?

Have you read these novels?

LE MASCULIN ET LE FÉMINIM DES MÉTIERS

THE MASCULINE AND FEMININE OF PROFESSIONS

In French, just like people, professions have genders. They are divided into sections depending on their endings.

AUDIO 3.1

Nouns ending in **-e** don't change.

Un architecte	**Une architecte**	*An architect*

For nouns ending in **-i**, **-é**, and **-t**, simply add **-e**.

Un apprenti	**Une apprentie**	*An apprentice*
Un associé	**Une associée**	*An associate*
Un avocat	**Une avocate**	*A lawyer*

For nouns ending in **-er**, the ending changes to **-ère**.

Un infirmier	**Une infirmière**	*A nurse*

For nouns ending in **-eur**, the ending changes to **-euse**.

Un coiffeur	**Une coiffeuse**	*A hairdresser*

For nouns ending in **-ien**, the ending changes to **-ienne**.

Un pharmacien	**Une pharmacienne**	*A pharmacist*

For nouns ending in **-on**, the ending changes to **-onne**.

Un patron	**Une patronne**	*A boss*

For nouns ending in -**teur**, the ending changes to **-trice**.

Un acteur	**Une actrice**	*An actor – An actress*

Ajoutez **le masculin** ou **le féminin** des métiers. Utilisez celui donné pour trouver celui qui manque.
Add the masculine or the feminine of the professions. Use the given one to find the missing one.

1. **Un** _____ – **Une factrice** livre le courrier et les colis.
   A postman – A postwoman delivers mail and packages.

2. **Un opticien – Une** _____ vérifie la vue de ses clients.
   An optician checks his/her clients' eyesight.

3. **Un** _____ – **Une boulangère** prépare des pains et des pâtisseries.
   A baker prepares breads and pastries.

4. **Un enseignant – Une** _____ donne des cours aux enfants.
   A teacher gives lessons to children.

5. **Un** _____ – **Une infirmière** prodigue des soins aux patients.
   A nurse provides care to patients.

6. **Un guide – Une** _____ accompagne les touristes.
   A guide accompanies the tourists.

7. **Un** _____ – **Une magicienne** réalise des tours de magie.
   A magician performs magic tricks.

8. **Un éducateur – Une** _____ travaille avec des enfants ou des adultes.
   An educator works with children or adults.

9. **Un** _____ – **Une reportrice** récolte des informations et réalise des interviews.
   A reporter collects information and conducts interviews.

10. **Un secrétaire – Une** _____ accomplit les tâches administratives.
    A secretary performs administrative tasks.

11. **Un** _____ – **Une dentiste** traite les problèmes dentaires.
    A dentist treats dental problems.

12. **Un avocat – Une**   représente ses clients au tribunal.

    A lawyer represents his/her clients in court.

13. **Un**   **– Une pharmacienne** prépare et vend des médicaments.

    A pharmacist prepares and sells medicines.

14. **Un acteur – Une**   joue des rôles pour des films ou des séries.

    An actor – An actress plays roles for films or series.

15. **Un**   **– Une étudiante** va à l'école tous les jours.

    A student goes to school every day.

LES NATIONALITÉS ET LES PAYS
NATIONALITIES AND COUNTRIES

4

Countries have genders in French. Most of the time, if a country ends in **-e**, it's a feminine country, besides **Le Mexique**. A few are also always plural.

Nationalities change for men and women, except when the nationality ends in **-e**. Let's see a short list of countries and their nationalities with their endings when masculine and feminine.

Important note: Nationalities in French only take a capital letter when they are nouns (preceded by **un** or **une**) but don't when they are adjectives (after **il est – elle est**).

AUDIO 4.1 ◄))

Un <u>F</u>rançais but **Il est <u>f</u>rançais.**

Nationalities ending in **-e** are the same for masculine and feminine.

AUDIO 4.2 ◄))

La Belgique – *Belgium*	**Un Belge**	**Une Belge**
La Suisse – *Switzerland*	**Un Suisse**	**Une Suisse**

Nationalities ending in **-ais** and **-ois** become **-aise** and **-oise**.

AUDIO 4.3 ◄))

L'Angleterre – *England*	**Un Anglais**	**Une Anglais<u>e</u>**
La France – *France*	**Un Français**	**Une Français<u>e</u>**
L'Irlande – *Ireland*	**Un Irlandais**	**Une Irlandais<u>e</u>**
Le Japon – *Japan*	**Un Japonais**	**Une Japonais<u>e</u>**
La Nouvelle-Zélande – *New Zealand*	**Un Néo-Zélandais**	**Une Néo-Zélandais<u>e</u>**
Les Pays-Bas – *Netherlands*	**Un Néerlandais**	**Une Néerlandais<u>e</u>**
La Pologne – *Poland*	**Un Polonais**	**Une Polonais<u>e</u>**
Le Portugal – *Portugal*	**Un Portugais**	**Une Portugais<u>e</u>**
Le Sénégal – *Senegal*	**Un Sénégalais**	**Une Sénégalais<u>e</u>**
La Chine – *China*	**Un Chinois**	**Une Chinois<u>e</u>**
Le Luxembourg – *Luxembourg*	**Un Luxembourgeois**	**Une Luxembourgeois<u>e</u>**

Nationalities ending in **-ien** become **-ienne**.

AUDIO 4.4 ◄))

L'Algérie – *Algeria*	Un Algérien	Une Algér**ienne**
L'Australie – *Australia*	Un Australien	Une Austral**ienne**
Le Brésil – *Brazil*	Un Brésilien	Une Brésil**ienne**
Le Canada – *Canada*	Un Canadien	Une Canad**ienne**
L'Inde – *India*	Un Indien	Une Ind**ienne**
L'Indonésie – *Indonesia*	Un Indonésien	Une Indonés**ienne**
L'Italie – *Italy*	Un Italien	Une Ital**ienne**
Le Vietnam – *Vietnam*	Un Vietnamien	Une Vietnam**ienne**

Nationalities ending in **-d** or **-l**, take an **-e**.

AUDIO 4.5 ◄))

L'Allemagne – *Germany*	Un Allemand	Une Allemand**e**
L'Espagne – *Spain*	Un Espagnol	Une Espagnol**e**

Nationalities ending in **-ain** and **-in** become **-aine** and **-ine**.

AUDIO 4.6 ◄))

Les États-Unis – *United States*	Un Américain	Une Améric**aine**
Le Maroc – *Morocco*	Un Marocain	Une Maroc**aine**
Le Mexique – *Mexico*	Un Mexicain	Une Mexic**aine**
Les Philippines – *Philippines*	Un Philippin	Une Philipp**ine**

AUDIO 4.7 ◄))

 Ajoutez **le pays** correspondant à chaque **nationalité** ou vice versa.
Add the country corresponding to each nationality or vice versa.

1. Cédric est _____ , il vient de **France**.
   Cédric is French, he comes from France.

2. Sarah est **algérienne**, elle vient d' _____ .
   Sarah is Algerian, she comes from Algeria.

3. Mon père est _____ , il vient du **Sénégal**.
   My father is Senegalese, he comes from Senegal.

4. Tu es **belge**, tu viens de   .

    You are Belgian, you come from Belgium.

5. Son professeur est   , il vient d'**Italie**.

    Her teacher is Italian, he comes from Italy.

6. Ma colocataire est **irlandaise**, elle vient d'   .

    My roommate is Irish, she comes from Ireland.

7. Mon collègue est   , il vient de **Suisse**.

    My colleague is Swiss, he comes from Switzerland.

8. Mon amie est **japonaise**, elle vient du   .

    My friend is Japanese, she comes from Japan.

9. Lisa est   , elle vient du **Canada**.

    Lisa is Canadian, she comes from Canada.

10. Mon patron est **vietnamien**, il vient du   .

    My boss is Vietnamese, he comes from Vietnam.

11. Jeff est   , il vient du **Maroc**.

    Jeff is Moroccan, he comes from Morocco.

12. Pedro est **portugais**, il vient du   .

    Pedro is Portuguese, he comes from Portugal.

13. Nora est   , elle vient d'**Inde**.

    Nora is Indian, she comes from India.

14. Cet auteur est **philippin**, il vient des   .

    This author is Filipino, he comes from the Philippines.

15. Le maire est   , il vient du **Luxembourg**.

    The mayor is Luxembourgish, he comes from Luxembourg.

LES PRONOMS SUJETS
SUBJECT PRONOUNS

What is a **subject pronoun**?

A **subject pronoun** is a word used to replace the subject of the sentence. Using pronouns helps you to avoid repetition.

French subject pronouns are:

AUDIO 5.1 🔊

Singular	Plural
Je – *I*	**Nous** – *We*
Tu – *You*	**Vous** – *You*
Il – *He*	**Ils** – *They (f)*
Elle – *She*	**Elles** – *They (m)*
On – *We (casual)*	

Je becomes **j'** when followed by a verb starting with a vowel or a silent h.

Tu is used to address a single person you are familiar with, such as a family member, a friend, a colleague, etc.

Il is only used for a masculine person or a masculine thing.

Elle is only used for a feminine person or a feminine thing.

On is often used to replace **nous**. It's a more casual way to speak. **On** is conjugated as if it were a singular subject.

Nous is used to talk about a group of people, including the person speaking.

Vous is used for a group of people or to address people you don't know or must show respect: a cashier, your teacher, your boss, etc.

Ils refers to a group of men or masculine things. But it can also refer to a group of mixed genders, as long as there is a man or a masculine thing in the group, we will use **ils**.

Elles only refers to a group of women or feminine things.

Note: Remember that inanimate objects also have genders in French, not only people. Gender neutral doesn't exist in French.

AUDIO 5.2 ◄ᴗ)

<u>Ma mère</u> est en retard = <u>Elle</u> est en retard.
My mother is late = She is late.

<u>La table</u> est cassée = <u>Elle</u> est cassée.
The table is broken = It is broken.

AUDIO 5.3 ◄ᴗ)

 Remplacez **le sujet** de la phrase par **un pronom sujet**.
Replace the subject of the sentence with a subject pronoun.

1. Julie et Anthony sont dans la même classe.
   Julie and Anthony are in the same class.

   _____ sont dans la même classe.

2. La souris est sur le bureau.
   The mouse is on the desk.

   _____ est sur le bureau.

3. Le ciel est couvert ce matin.
   The sky is overcast this morning.

   _____ est couvert ce matin.

4. Mon passeport est dans le coffre-fort.
   My passport is in the safe.

   _____ est dans le coffre-fort.

5. Flore et moi serons en congé en même temps.
   Flore and I will be off at the same time.

   _____ serons en congé en même temps.

6. Attention, la poêle est très chaude.
   Be careful, the pan is very hot.

   Attention, _____ est très chaude.

7. Ton frère et toi devriez regarder ce film.
   You and your brother should watch this movie.

   _____ devriez regarder ce film.

8. La piscine sera fermée samedi.
The swimming pool will be closed on Saturday.

                    sera fermée samedi.

9. Malheureusement, mon fils n'a pas réussi son permis de conduire.
Unfortunately, my son did not pass his driving test.

Malheureusement,   n'a pas réussi son permis de conduire.

10. Ma voisine sera à la retraite dans quelques mois.
My neighbor will be retired in a few months.

                    sera à la retraite dans quelques mois.

11. Le lait est périmé.
The milk is expired.

                    est périmé.

12. Sa montre est en panne pour la deuxième fois.
His watch broke for the second time.

                    est en panne pour la deuxième fois.

13. Lina et Pascal sont allergiques aux œufs.
Lina and Pascal are allergic to eggs.

                    sont allergiques aux œufs.

14. Mon professeur est vraiment passionné par son travail.
My teacher is really passionate about his work.

                    est vraiment passionné par son travail.

15. La tempête a déjà commencé.
The storm has already started.

                    a déjà commencé.

LA CONJUGAISON D'ÊTRE
THE CONJUGATION OF ÊTRE

> **Être** (*to be*) is one of the most common French verbs with **avoir** (*to have*). They are both used in expressions, as auxiliaries, and as regular verbs.

We are going to see **avoir** in chapter 14 but in the meantime, let's review **être** with its irregular conjugation and practice with an exercise.

Note: You should learn the conjugation of irregular French verbs by heart.

Présent de l'indicatif

AUDIO 6.1 ◀))

Je suis – *I am*
Tu es – *You are*
Il-Elle est – *He-She is*
On est – *We are*
Nous sommes – *We are*
Vous êtes – *You are*
Ils-Elles sont – *They are*

Passé composé

AUDIO 6.2 ◀))

J'ai été – *I have been*
Tu as été – *You have been*
Il-Elle a été – *He-She has been*
On a été – *We have been*
Nous avons été – *We have been*
Vous avez été – *You have been*
Ils-Elles ont été – *They have been*

Imparfait

AUDIO 6.3 ◀))

J'étais – *I was*
Tu étais – *You were*
Il-Elle était – *He-She was*
On était – *We were*
Nous étions – *We were*
Vous étiez – *You were*
Ils-Elles étaient – *They were*

Futur simple

AUDIO 6.4 ◀))

Je serai – *I will be*
Tu seras – *You will be*
Il-Elle sera – *He-She will be*
On sera – *We will be*
Nous serons – *We will be*
Vous serez – *You will be*
Ils-Elles seront – *They will be*

Conditionnel présent

AUDIO 6.5 ◀))

Je serais – *I would be*
Tu serais – *You would be*
Il-Elle serait – *He-She would be*
On serait – *We would be*
Nous serions – *We would be*
Vous seriez – *You would be*
Ils-Elles seraient – *They would be*

Subjonctif présent

AUDIO 6.6 ◀))

Que je sois – *That I am*
Que tu sois – *That you are*
Qu'il-elle soit – *That he-she is*
Qu'on soit – *That we are*
Que nous soyons – *That we are*
Que vous soyez – *That you are*
Qu'ils-elles soient – *That they are*

Futur proche

AUDIO 6.7

Je vais être – *I am going to be*
Tu vas être – *You are going to be*
Il-Elle va être – *He-She is going to be*
On va être – *We are going to be*
Nous allons être – *We are going to be*
Vous allez être – *You are going to be*
Ils-Elles vont être – *They are going to be*

Passé récent

AUDIO 6.8

Je viens d'être – *I have just been*
Tu viens d'être – *You have just been*
Il-Elle vient d'être – *He-She has just been*
On vient d'être – *We have just been*
Nous venons d'être – *We have just been*
Vous venez d'être – *You have just been*
Ils-Elles viennent d'être – *They have just been*

Impératif

AUDIO 6.9

Sois ! – *Be!*
Soyons ! – *Let's be!*
Soyez ! – *Be!*

AUDIO 6.10

 Conjuguez le verbe **être** au temps donné. Essayez de regarder le tableau de conjugaison avant et de compléter l'exercice de mémoire.
Conjugate the verb être in the given tense. Try to look at the conjugation chart before and complete the exercise by memory.

1. **Présent de l'indicatif** : Je _____ étudiant.
    I am a student.

2. **Imparfait x2** : Quand on _____ jeunes, on _____ timides.
    When we were young, we were shy.

3. **Futur simple** : Demain, il _____ à Paris pour son concert.
    Tomorrow, he will be in Paris for his concert.

4. **Passé composé** : J' _____ malade après le repas.
    I was sick after the meal.

5. **Impératif** : _____ prudent quand tu conduis !
    Be careful when you drive!

6. **Conditionnel présent** : Je ne sais pas si je _____ plus heureux avec plus d'argent.

   I don't know if I would be happier with more money.

7. **Subjonctif présent** : Il faut que tu _____ là pour signer les documents.

   You have to be there to sign the documents.

8. **Imparfait** : Si tu _____ ici, tu comprendrais.

   If you were here, you would understand.

9. **Passé récent** : Je _____ élu maire de la ville.

   I have just been elected mayor of the city.

10. **Futur proche** : Elle _____ diplômée dans quelques semaines.

    She is going to graduate in a few weeks.

11. **Passé composé** : Elle _____ surprise par le résultat du match.

    She was surprised by the result of the match.

12. **Imparfait - Conditionnel présent** : Si j' _____ toi, je _____ plus attentif pendant les cours.

    If I were you, I would be more attentive during lessons.

13. **Futur simple** : Demain, nous _____ enfin en vacances.

    Tomorrow we will finally be on vacation.

14. **Présent de l'indicatif** : Pourquoi est-ce que tu n' _____ pas d'accord ?

    Why don't you agree?

15. **Conditionnel présent** : Tu ne _____ pas en retard si tu t'étais réveillé à l'heure.

    You wouldn't be late if you had woken up on time.

TROUVEZ LES ERREURS

FIND THE ERRORS

7

Time for a recap! Here are 15 questions related to everything we have seen from chapter 1 to the last chapter. Each answer is explained in the solutions.

AUDIO 7.1 ◄))

 Trouvez **les erreurs** dans les phrases ci-dessous. Complétez l'exercice avant d'écouter l'audio.
Find the errors in the sentences below. Complete the exercise before listening to the audio.

1. Il travaille seul, il n'a pas des collègues.
   He works alone, he has no colleagues.

2. Les enfant ont un anniversaire ce samedi.
   The children have a birthday this Saturday.

3. Je pense qu'il est canadienne mais je ne suis pas certaine.
   I think he's Canadian but I'm not sure.

4. Le client n'est pas content. Elle dit que les légumes ne sont pas frais.
   The customer is not happy. He says the vegetables are not fresh.

5. Elle mange une pomme et poire.
   She eats an apple and a pear.

6. Il s'est fait mal aux genous.
   He hurt his knees.

7. Le vétérinair soigne les animaux.
   The veterinarian treats the animals.

8. Marie est français mais elle habite aux États-Unis.
Marie is French but she lives in the United States.

9. J'ai bu une café après le repas.
I had a coffee after the meal.

10. J'attends un appel de mon avocatrice.
I'm waiting for a call from my lawyer.

11. Il faut qu'on sois prêts pour la réception.
We have to be ready for the reception.

12. J' viens juste de partir.
I just left.

13. Les prixs augmentent constamment.
Prices are constantly increasing.

14. Est-ce que tu es déjà allé en inde ?
Have you ever been to India?

15. Je ne sera pas là quand tu arrives.
I won't be there when you arrive.

LE – LA – L' – LES
THE

8

Le, la, l', and **les** *(the)* are definite articles in French. They change depending on if the noun is masculine, feminine, singular, or plural. We use them to talk about **specific things** or **people**. When a word starts with a vowel or a silent h, **le** and **la** become **l'**.

AUDIO 8.1 ◀》

	Masculine	Feminine
Singular	**Le - L'** – *The*	**La - L'** – *The*
	Le thé – *The tea*	**La lampe** – *The lamp*
	L'orage – *The thunder*	**L'orange** – *The orange*
Plural	**Les** – *The*	**Les** – *The*
	Les thés – *Teas*	**Les lampes** – *Lamps*
	Les orages – *Thunders*	**Les oranges** – *Oranges*

One thing that is different between French and English, is that French almost always uses definite articles while English doesn't always use them.

AUDIO 8.2 ◀》

J'étudie le français depuis deux ans.

I have been studying French for two years.

———————————

AUDIO 8.3 ◀》

 Ajoutez **le, la, l'** ou **les** aux phrases suivantes. Attention, parfois deux articles peuvent être utilisés.

Add le, la, l' or les to the following sentences. Please note, sometimes two articles can be used.

1. Je n'ai pas enregistré   document avant de fermer ordinateur.

    I did not save the document before closing the computer.

2. Est-ce que tu as goûté   pain ?

    Have you tasted the bread?

3. _____ pays traverse une situation économique difficile.

The country is going through a difficult economic situation.

4. Elle fait tremper _____ pois chiches pendant des heures.

She soaks the chickpeas for hours.

5. _____ ministre a un rendez-vous avec _____ journalistes.

The minister has a meeting with journalists.

6. _____ crise a été évitée de peu.

The crisis was narrowly averted.

7. Parfois, on peut voir _____ raton laveur qui vit dans _____ jardin.

Sometimes we can see the raccoon that lives in the garden.

8. Il adore _____ mode.

He loves fashion.

9. _____ année a été difficile pour _____ fermiers.

It's been a tough year for farmers.

10. _____ jour où tu es né était _____ plus beau jour de ma vie.

The day you were born was the happiest day of my life.

11. _____ prix va diminuer dans _____ prochains jours.

The price will decrease in the coming days.

12. Tu te souviens de _____ fois où il est tombé dans _____ escaliers ?

Do you remember that time he fell down the stairs?

13. _____ homme que j'ai vu ne ressemblait pas à ce portrait.

The man I saw did not look like this portrait.

14. _____ chien des voisins se sauve souvent.

The neighbors' dog often runs away.

15. _____ question qu'il a posée est une bonne question.

The question he asked is a good question.

LE – LA – L' – LES & UN – UNE – DES
THE & A

In chapter 1 and chapter 8, we saw **un – une – des** and **le – la – l' – les**. Seeing them separately is relatively easy so let's do an exercise with both.

But first, a quick review!

Un – Une – Des are used to talk about **unspecified things** or **people**.

AUDIO 9.1 🔊

	Masculine	Feminine
Singular	**Un** – *A* **Un chien** – *A dog*	**Une** – *A* **Une maison** – *A house*
Plural	**Des** – *Some/any* **Des chiens** – *Dogs*	**Des** – *Some/any* **Des maisons** – *Houses*

Le – La – L' – Les are used to talk about **specific things** or **people**.

AUDIO 9.2 🔊

	Masculine	Feminine
Singular	**Le – L'**- *The* **Le thé** – *The tea* **L'orage** – *The thunder*	**La – L'**- *The* **La lampe** – *The lamp* **L'orange** – *The orange*
Plural	**Les** – *The* **Les thés** – *Teas* **Les orages** – *Thunders*	**Les** – *The* **Les lampes** – *Lamps* **Les oranges** – *Oranges*

AUDIO 9.3 🔊

 Ajoutez **un, une, des** ou **le, la, l', les** aux phrases suivantes. Regardez à la traduction pour vous aider.
Add un, une, des ou le, la, l', les to the following sentences. Look to the translation to help you.

1. Il y a _____ avion dans _____ ciel.

   There is a plane in the sky.

---

2. J'ai commandé   livre dont tu m'as parlé.

I ordered the book you told me about.

3. Est-ce que tu veux regarder   film ce soir ?

Do you want to watch a movie tonight?

4. Je suis certaine que   voiture que j'ai vue était noire.

I'm sure the car I saw was black.

5. Il y a   oiseaux qui chantent dans   arbre.

There are birds singing in the tree.

6.   fleurs de ton jardin sont magnifiques.

The flowers in your garden are beautiful.

7.   femme que j'ai rencontrée au supermarché était très gentille.

The woman I met at the supermarket was very nice.

8.   étoiles brillent pendant   nuit.

The stars shine at night.

9.   de mes amies vient de se marier.

One of my friends just got married.

10. Mon chien aboie après   souris.

My dog barks at a mouse.

11. On a vu   ours durant notre voyage au Canada.

We saw a bear during our trip to Canada.

12.   clients font   queue pour attendre leur tour.

Customers line up to wait their turn.

13. J'ai envie de faire   sieste.

I want to take a nap.

14. Est-ce que tu as   temps de discuter un peu ?

Do you have time to chat a little?

15.   appartement se trouve au deuxième étage.

The apartment is on the second floor.

LA CONJUGAISON DES VERBES PRONOMINAUX

10

THE CONJUGATION OF REFLEXIVE VERBS

Reflexive verbs are common in French and can be found in everyday conversations. Their conjugation, while being similar to regular verbs, is also different.

What is a Reflexive Verb?

In French, a reflexive verb is a verb indicating that the action is being performed on the subject. There are similar verbs in English, such as *"To burn yourself* – **Se brûler**".

In French, a reflexive verb is called **un verbe pronominal** because it includes a pronoun (pronom). The infinitive of a reflexive verb is always **se** + verb, or **s'** + verb if the verb starts with a vowel or a silent h. **Se** is the pronoun.

se + verb

se réveiller = to wake up

How to Conjugate a Reflexive Verb?

When a reflexive verb is conjugated, it's a mix of a simple verb with an extra pronoun. The extra pronoun is always placed before the verb. The verb follows the same conjugation as regular verbs.

The pronouns are:

AUDIO 10.1 ◀))

Subject pronouns	Reflexive pronouns
Je	me – m'
Tu	te – t'
Il-Elle-On	se – s'
Nous	nous
Vous	vous
Ils-Elles	se – s'

Remember that in the case of **me**, **te** and **se**, if the verb starts with a vowel or a silent h, we use **m'**, **t'**, **s'**.

Regular verb	Reflexive verb

AUDIO 10.2 ◀))   AUDIO 10.3 ◀))

Demander – *To ask*	**Se demander** – *To ask yourself/To wonder*
Je demande – *I ask*	**Je me demande** – *I wonder*
Tu demandes – *You ask*	**Tu te demandes** – *You wonder*
Il-Elle demande – *He-She asks*	**Il-Elle se demande** – *He-She wonders*
On demande – *We ask*	**On se demande** – *We wonder*
Nous demandons – *We ask*	**Nous nous demandons** – *We wonder*
Vous demandez – *You ask*	**Vous vous demandez** – *You wonder*
Ils-Elles demandent – *They ask*	**Ils-Elles se demandent** – *They wonder*

AUDIO 10.4 ◀))

 Conjuguez **le verbe** donné au **présent de l'indicatif**. N'oubliez pas d'ajouter le bon pronom pronominal.
Conjugate the given verb in the present tense. Don't forget to add the right reflexive pronoun.

1. **Se demander** – Je _____ comment il va.
   I wonder how he is doing.

2. **S'excuser** – Il _____ toujours trop tard.
   He always apologizes too late.

3. **S'amuser** – Les enfants _____ dans le jardin.
   The children are having fun in the garden.

4. **Se maquiller** – Elle _____ avant de s'habiller.
   She puts on makeup before getting dressed.

5. **Se promener** – Les touristes _____ toujours dans cette partie de la ville.
   Tourists always walk around this part of town.

6. **Se réveiller** – On _____ tous les jours à 6 heures.
   We wake up every day at 6 a.m.

7. **Se préparer** – Ils _____ pour sortir.

They are getting ready to go out.

8. **Se laver** – Je _____ le soir au lieu du matin.

I shower in the evening instead of in the morning.

9. **Se marier** – Ils _____ ce matin à la mairie.

They are getting married this morning at the town hall.

10. **S'habiller** – Mon fils _____ seul depuis quelques temps.

My son has been dressing himself for some time now.

11. **Se comporter** – Le chien _____ bizarrement.

The dog is acting strange.

12. **Se brosser** – Je _____ les dents trois fois par jour.

I brush my teeth three times a day.

13. **Se reposer** – Mon père _____ dans le canapé.

My father is resting on the sofa.

14. **S'adapter** – Ma fille _____ assez vite à sa nouvelle école.

My daughter adapts quite quickly to her new school.

15. **S'habituer** – Je _____ doucement à mon nouvel appareil dentaire.

I'm slowly getting used to my new braces.

VERBES PRONOMINAUX OU VERBES RÉGULIERS

11

REFLEXIVE VERBS OR REGULAR VERBS

In the last exercise, we saw what a reflexive verb is as well as the conjugation of reflexive verbs in the present tense. In this exercise, we are going to learn the difference between reflexive verbs and regular verbs. Which one to choose?

Differences Between a Regular and a Reflexive Verb

Many reflexive verbs and regular verbs have the same meaning, just that the reflexive verb refers to the person or the object. A good way to see the difference is to add **quelque chose** *(something)* or **quelqu'un** *(someone)* after the verb. If the sentence works, it's a regular verb, if it doesn't work, it's a reflexive verb. As you can see below, the translation of the reflexive verb can be followed by "*yourself*" since it refers to the subject.

AUDIO 11.1 ◄))

Regular verb:
Regarder quelque chose – *To watch something*
Il regarde la télévision. *He is watching TV.*

Appeler quelqu'un – *To call someone*
J'appelle mon frère. *I am calling my brother.*

Reflexive verb:
Se regarder – *To look at **yourself***
Il se regarde dans le miroir. *He is looking at himself in the mirror.*

AUDIO 11.2 ◄))

 Choisissez le bon verbe entre **le verbe régulier** ou **le verbe pronominal** et conjuguez-le au présent de l'indicatif.
Choose the right verb between regular verb and reflexive verb and conjugate it in the present tense.

1. **Promener – Se promener –** On _____ le chien au parc.
    To walk – To take a walk – *We are walking the dog at the park.*

2. **Maquiller – Se maquiller –** Est-ce que tu _____ tous les jours ?
    To do someone's makeup – To put on makeup – *Do you put on makeup every day?*

---

3. **Appeler – S'appeler** – Je _____ Dylane, et toi ?

    To call – To be named – My name is Dylane, and you?

4. **Demander – Se demander** – L'élève _____ de l'aide au professeur.

    To ask – To wonder – The student is asking the teacher for help.

5. **Épiler – S'épiler** – Je ne _____ pas toutes les semaines.

    To wax – To wax yourself – I don't wax every week.

6. **Couper – Se couper** – Elle _____ les légumes pour le dîner.

    To cut – To cut yourself – She is cutting the vegetables for dinner.

7. **Perdre – Se perdre** – On _____ toujours quand on voyage.

    To lose – To get lost – We always get lost when we travel.

8. **Tromper – Se tromper** – Je ne le savais pas mais il _____ sa femme.

    To cheat on – To make a mistake – I didn't know it but he is cheating on his wife.

9. **Appuyer – S'appuyer** – Le petit garçon _____ sur le bouton de l'ascenseur.

    To press – To lean – The little boy presses the elevator button.

10. **Rappeler – Se rappeler** – Je _____ ce client tout de suite.

    To call back – To remember – I will call this customer back right away.

11. **Sécher – Se sécher** – Le linge _____ dans le jardin.

    To dry – To dry yourself – The laundry is drying in the garden.

12. **Changer – Se changer** – Je _____ car mon pull est taché.

    To change – To get changed – I'm getting changed because my sweater is stained.

13. **Inquiéter – S'inquiéter** – Elle _____ beaucoup pour son avenir.

    To worry – To worry yourself – She worries a lot about her future.

14. **Conduire – Se conduire** – Ma voisine _____ son mari au travail tous les jours.

    To drive – To behave – My neighbor drives her husband to work every day.

15. **Asseoir – S'asseoir** – Ça va pour toi si on _____ ici ?

    To sit – To sit yourself/To sit down – Is it okay for you if we sit here?

LES VERBES PRONOMINAUX
ET LES PARTIES DU CORPS

12

REFLEXIVE VERBS AND BODY PARTS

A big difference between French and English is that in French,
we don't use possessive adjectives *(my, your, etc.)* to talk about body parts. Instead,
we use definite articles **le, la, l', les** *(the)*.

The reason behind this rule is pretty simple, reflexive verbs already refer to the subject,
adding possessive adjectives would result in a double possessive.

AUDIO 12.1 ◄))

Je me rase <u>la</u> barbe. *I am shaving my beard.*
Elle s'épile <u>les</u> sourcils. *She is plucking her eyebrows.*

Here is the list of the most common ones:

AUDIO 12.2 ◄))

S'épiler <u>les</u> sourcils	*To pluck your eyebrows*
S'essuyer <u>les</u> pieds	*To wipe your feet*
Se brosser <u>les</u> cheveux	*To brush your hair*
Se brosser <u>les</u> dents	*To brush your teeth*
Se casser <u>le</u> pied	*To break your foot*
Se couper <u>les</u> ongles	*To cut your nails*
Se fouler <u>la</u> cheville	*To sprain your ankle*
Se laver <u>les</u> mains	*To wash your hands*
Se limer <u>les</u> ongles	*To file your nails*
Se peigner <u>les</u> cheveux	*To comb your hair*
Se raser <u>la</u> barbe	*To shave your beard*
Se sécher <u>les</u> cheveux	*To dry your hair*

AUDIO 12.3 ◄))

Ajoutez **le bon article** après chaque **verbe pronominal**.
Add the right article after each reflexive verb.

1. Il se rase _____ barbe tous les jours.

He shaves his beard every day.

---

2. Est-ce te tu t'es peigné   cheveux ?

Did you comb your hair?

3. Il faut se laver   mains plusieurs fois par jour.

You should wash your hands several times a day.

4. N'oublie pas de te sécher   cheveux.

Don't forget to dry your hair.

5. Elle s'est cassé   pied il y a plusieurs années.

She broke her foot several years ago.

6. Je dois me limer   ongles mais je ne trouve pas ma lime.

I need to file my nails but I can't find my file.

7. Une personne s'est foulé   cheville en sortant du restaurant.

A person sprained their ankle leaving the restaurant.

8. C'est important de se brosser   cheveux tous les jours.

It's important to brush your hair every day.

9. Merci de vous essuyer   pieds.

Please dry your feet.

10. Je n'ai pas toujours le temps de m'épiler   sourcils.

I don't always have time to pluck my eyebrows.

CE – CET – CETTE – CES
THIS – THAT – THESE – THOSE

13

Ce, cet, cette, and **ces** are demonstrative adjectives. They are the equivalent of *this/that* and *these/those* in English. They are placed before a noun or sometimes before an adjective.

2 Simple Rules to Remember:

- French demonstrative adjectives agree with what they describe and therefore take the gender and number of the following noun.
- When a masculine, singular noun or adjective starts with a vowel or a silent h, we will use **cet** and not **ce**.

AUDIO 13.1 ◀))

CE – *This/That*

Use **ce** before a masculine noun or adjective starting with a consonant.

Ce film – *This/That movie*
Ce chien – *This/That dog*

CET – *This/That*

Use **cet** before a masculine noun or adjective starting with a vowel or a silent h.

Cet arbre – *This/That tree*
Cet homme – *This/That man*

CETTE – *This/That*

Use **cette** before a feminine noun.

Cette histoire – *This/That story*
Cette voiture – *This/That car*

CES – *These/Those*

Use **ces** before a plural noun.

Ces papiers – *These/Those papers*
Ces voitures – *These/Those cars*

Ajoutez **ce – cet – cette – ces** dans chaque phrase.
Add ce – cet – cette – ces in each sentence.

1. _____ robe est superbe. Elle te va très bien.
    This dress is superb. It fits you very well.

2. Tu as vu _____ nouvel article dans le journal ?
    Have you seen this new article in the newspaper?

3. _____ fleurs sentent vraiment bon.
    These flowers smell really good.

4. _____ exercice est un peu trop facile pour moi.
    This exercise is a bit too easy for me.

5. C'est _____ voiture que je voulais acheter.
    It's this car that I wanted to buy.

6. _____ appartement est trop petit pour nous.
    This apartment is too small for us.

7. Est-ce que _____ stylo est à toi ?
    Is this pen yours?

8. _____ homme ressemble beaucoup à mon père.
    This man looks a lot like my father.

9. _____ montagne est dangereuse pour les skieurs.
    This mountain is dangerous for skiers.

10. Fais attention, _____ café est très chaud.
    Be careful, this coffee is very hot.

11. J'ai beaucoup aimé _____ chanson.
    I really liked this song.

12. _____ ordinateur tombe toujours en panne.
    This computer always breaks down.

13. _____ chaise n'est pas confortable du tout.

This chair is not comfortable at all.

14. Beaucoup de gens se perdent dans _____ parc.

Many people get lost in this park.

15. _____ plantes que tu as achetées sont magnifiques.

These plants you bought are beautiful.

LA CONJUGAISON D'AVOIR
THE CONJUGATION OF AVOIR

14

As we saw in chapter 6 with **être**, **avoir** *(to have)* is another French verb that is used in expressions, as auxiliaries, and as regular verbs. Let's review **avoir** with its irregular conjugation and practice with an exercise.

Note: You should learn the conjugation of irregular French verbs by heart.

Présent de l'indicatif

AUDIO 14.1 ◀))

J'ai – *I have*
Tu as – *You have*
Il-Elle a – *He-She has*
On a – *We have*
Nous avons – *We have*
Vous avez – *You have*
Ils-Elles ont – *They have*

Passé composé

AUDIO 14.2 ◀))

J'ai eu – *I have had*
Tu as eu – *You have had*
Il-Elle a eu – *He-She has had*
On a eu – *We have had*
Nous avons eu – *We have had*
Vous avez eu – *You have had*
Ils-Elles ont eu – *They have had*

Imparfait

AUDIO 14.3 ◀))

J'avais – *I had*
Tu avais – *You had*
Il-Elle avait – *He-She had*
On avait – *We had*
Nous avions – *We had*
Vous aviez – *You had*
Ils-Elles avaient – *They had*

Futur simple

AUDIO 14.4 ◀))

J'aurai – *I will have*
Tu auras – *You will have*
Il-Elle aura – *He-She will have*
On aura – *We will have*
Nous aurons – *We will have*
Vous aurez – *You will have*
Ils-Elles auront – *They will have*

Conditionnel présent

AUDIO 14.5 ◀))

J'aurais – *I would have*
Tu aurais – *You would have*
Il-Elle aurait – *He-She would have*
On aurait – *We would have*
Nous aurions – *We would have*
Vous auriez – *You would have*
Ils-Elles auraient – *They would have*

Subjonctif présent

AUDIO 14.6 ◀))

Que j'aie – *That I have*
Que tu aies – *That you have*
Qu'il-elle ait – *That he-she has*
Qu'on ait – *That we have*
Que nous ayons – *That we have*
Que vous ayez – *That you have*
Qu'ils-elles aient – *That they have*

Futur proche

AUDIO 14.7

Je vais avoir – *I am going to have*
Tu vas avoir – *You are going to have*
Il-Elle va avoir – *He-She is going to have*
On va avoir – *We are going to have*
Nous allons avoir – *We are going to have*
Vous allez avoir – *You are going to have*
Ils-Elles vont avoir – *They are going to have*

Passé récent

AUDIO 14.8

Je viens d'avoir – *I just had*
Tu viens d'avoir – *You just had*
Il-Elle vient d'avoir – *He-She just had*
On vient d'avoir – *We just had*
Nous venons d'avoir – *We just had*
Vous venez d'avoir – *You just had*
Ils-Elles viennent d'avoir – *They just had*

Impératif

AUDIO 14.9

Aie ! – *Have!*
Ayons ! – *Let's have!*
Ayez ! – *Have!*

AUDIO 14.10

 Conjuguez le verbe **avoir** au temps donné. Essayez de regarder le tableau de conjugaison avant et de compléter l'exercice de mémoire.
Conjugate the verb avoir in the given tense. Try to look at the conjugation chart before and complete the exercise by memory.

1. **Présent de l'indicatif :** J'   un chien et deux chats.
   I have a dog and two cats.

2. **Futur simple :** Demain, on   nos résultats.
   Tomorrow, we will have our results.

3. **Passé composé :** Hier, elle   une idée de génie.
   Yesterday, she had a genius idea.

4. **Impératif :**   confiance en toi !
   Have confidence in yourself!

5. **Futur simple :** Mes parents   leur nouvelle voiture quand on les verra.
   My parents will have their new car when we see them.

---

6. **Subjonctif présent** : Il faut que tu   plus de points pour réussir.

   You need to have more points to pass.

7. **Présent de l'indicatif** : Le secrétaire   le temps de remplir les documents.

   The secretary has time to complete the documents.

8. **Imparfait** : J'   un vélo comme celui-ci quand j'étais petite.

   I had a bike like this when I was little.

9. **Passé composé** : Il   ce qu'il voulait.

   He got what he wanted.

10. **Passé récent** : Mon ami   son permis de conduire.

    My friend just had his driving license.

11. **Subjonctif présent** : Il faut que le passager   son billet pour monter dans l'avion.

    The passenger must have his ticket to board the plane.

12. **Futur simple** : Demain, nous   finalement les clés de notre nouvelle maison.

    Tomorrow we will finally have the keys to our new house.

13. **Présent de l'indicatif** : Est-ce que tu   un peu de temps pour moi ?

    Do you have some time for me?

14. **Futur proche** : Mon frère et sa femme   un bébé dans les prochains jours.

    My brother and his wife are going to have a baby in the next few days.

15. **Passé composé** : Il   un accident de voiture hier soir mais il va bien.

    He had a car accident last night, but he is fine.

LES EXPRESSIONS AVEC AVOIR ET ÊTRE

15

EXPRESSIONS WITH AVOIR AND ÊTRE

Être and **avoir** are the two most used verbs in French as we have seen in this book. They are both irregulars and should be known by heart. They are also used as auxiliaries in compound tenses like **passé composé**.

Here are **être** and **avoir** conjugated in the present tense.

AUDIO 15.1 ◄))

Être – *To be*

Je suis – *I am*
Tu es – *You are*
Il est – *He is*
Elle est – *She is*
On est – *We are*
Nous sommes – *We are*
Vous êtes – *You are*
Ils sont – *They are (m)*
Elles sont – *They are (f)*

Avoir – *To have*

J'ai – *I have*
Tu as – *You have*
Il a – *He has*
Elle a – *She has*
On a – *We have*
Nous avons – *We have*
Vous avez – *You have*
Ils ont – *They have (m)*
Elles ont – *They have (f)*

Since **être** and **avoir** are the most used French verbs, they are also the most used in French expressions. Here are 15 common French expressions with each verb.

AUDIO 15.2 ◄))

15 Common French Expressions with Être – *To be*

Être + nationality	*To be + nationality*
Être à quelqu'un	*To belong to somebody*
Être à l'heure	*To be on time*
Être au courant	*To be informed*
Être de	*To be from*
Être de bonne humeur	*To be in a good mood*
Être de retour	*To be back*
Être en avance	*To be early*
Être en bonne santé	*To be healthy*

Être en retard	*To be late*
Être en train de (+ inf)	*To be in the process of (doing)*
Être né(e)	*To be born*
Être prêt(e)	*To be ready*
Être sur le point de (+ inf)	*To be about to (do)*
C'est / Ce sont	*It is/He is/They are*

15 Common French Expressions with Avoir – To have

French expressions with **Avoir** often translate to *To be* in English.

Avoir … ans	*To be … years old*
Avoir besoin de	*To need*
Avoir confiance en	*To trust*
Avoir chaud	*To be hot*
Avoir de la chance	*To be lucky*
Avoir envie de	*To want*
Avoir faim	*To be hungry*
Avoir froid	*To be cold*
Avoir hâte de	*Can't wait to*
Avoir horreur de	*To hate*
Avoir mal	*To be in pain*
Avoir l'impression que	*To be under the impression that*
Avoir peur (de)	*To be afraid (of)*
Avoir soif	*To be thirsty*
Avoir sommeil	*To be sleepy*

 Ajoutez le verbe **être** ou **avoir** conjugué au présent dans chaque phrase.
Add the verb être or avoir conjugated in the present tense in each sentence.

1. J' _____ tellement faim !

   I'm so hungry!

2. Tu _____ né le même jour que moi.

   You were born on the same day as me.

3. Son sac à main _____ noir.

   Her handbag is black.

4. Mets un pull si tu   froid.

   Put on a sweater if you're cold.

5. Je pense qu'il   prêt pour son examen.

   I think he's ready for his exam.

6. On   hâte de partir en vacances.

   We can't wait to go on vacation.

7. Nous   en train de préparer le dîner.

   We are preparing dinner.

8. Il   en route mais il sera en retard.

   He's on his way but he will be late.

9. Elle   vraiment besoin de se reposer.

   She really needs to rest.

10. Mon oncle n'   pas en bonne santé.

    My uncle is not in good health.

11. J'   mal aux dents mais je ne veux pas aller chez le dentiste.

    My teeth hurt but I don't want to go to the dentist.

12. Est-ce que tu   peur du noir ?

    Are you afraid of the dark?

13. Elle   de bonne humeur aujourd'hui.

    She's in a good mood today.

14. J'   toujours de la chance quand je joue à la loterie.

    I am always lucky when I play the lottery.

15. C'   une personne très gentille.

    He is a very kind person.

MON MA MES – TON TA TES – SON SA SES

16

MY – YOUR – HIS HER ITS

> **Mon ma mes** *(my)*, **ton ta tes** *(your)*, **son sa ses** *(his/her/its)* are French possessive adjectives. They are used the same way as in English. They can be followed by a noun or an adjective.

In chapter 18, we will see **notre notre nos, votre votre vos, leur leur leurs** which are the plural French possessive adjectives.

2 simple rules to remember:

- French possessive adjectives agree in gender and number with the noun they preceed.
- When a feminine noun or adjective starts with a vowel or a silent h, we use "**mon – ton – son**".

	Masculine or feminine starting with a vowel or a silent h	Feminine	Plural
My	**mon**	**ma**	**mes**
Your	**ton**	**ta**	**tes**
His/Her/Its	**son**	**sa**	**ses**

AUDIO 16.1 ◄))

MON – MA – MES – *My*

Mon téléphone est déchargé. *My phone is out of charge.*
Ma mère vient de m'appeler. *My mother just called me.*
Mon écharpe est sale. *My scarf is dirty.*
Mes parents arrivent. *My parents are arriving.*

TON – TA – TES – *Your*

Ton téléphone est déchargé. *Your phone is out of charge.*
Ta mère vient de m'appeler. *Your mother just called me.*
Ton écharpe est sale. *Your scarf is dirty.*
Tes parents arrivent. *Your parents are arriving.*

SON – SA – SES – *His/Her/Its*

Son téléphone est déchargé. *His/Her phone is out of charge.*
Sa mère vient de m'appeler. *His/Her mother just called me.*
Son écharpe est sale. *His/Her scarf is dirty.*
Ses parents arrivent. *His/Her parents are arriving.*

AUDIO 16.2 🔊

 Ajoutez **mon ma mes – ton ta tes – son sa ses** à chaque phrase. Regardez à la traduction pour vous aider.
Add mon ma mes – ton ta tes – son sa ses to each sentence. Look to the translation to help you.

1. Est-ce que c'est _____ livre sur la table ?
   Is that your book on the table?

2. _____ maison est vraiment jolie mais elle est un peu grande.
   Her house is really pretty but it's a bit big.

3. _____ lunettes sont de travers.
   Your glasses are crooked.

4. Comment se sont passées _____ vacances ?
   How were his holidays?

5. Tous _____ rendez-vous ont été annulés.
   All my appointments were canceled.

6. Fais _____ devoirs avant d'aller jouer.
   Do your homework before going to play.

7. _____ école va être rénovée pendant les vacances d'été.
   My school is going to be renovated during the summer holidays.

8. Est-ce que _____ voiture est finalement réparée ?
   Has your car finally been repaired?

9. Il laisse toujours _____ jouets partout dans la maison.
   He always leaves his toys everywhere in the house.

---

10. _____ mère ne pourra pas être là à la remise des clés.

My mother won't be able to be there for the key handover.

11. Elle a encore oublié _____ sac dans le train.

She forgot her bag on the train again.

12. _____ cours commencent à quelle heure ?

What time do your classes start?

13. _____ ordinateur est branché mais il ne s'allume pas.

His computer is plugged in but it won't turn on.

14. _____ habits sont toujours dans le sèche-linge.

My clothes are still in the dryer.

15. _____ horaire est affiché dans la classe.

Your schedule is displayed in the classroom.

CES OU SES ?
CES OR SES?

17

Ses and ces are pronounced the same way in French but they have different meanings!
Let's review what we saw earlier in this book and practice them in context.

In chapter 13, we saw that **ces** is a demonstrative adjective. It means *these/those*. It's the plural of **ce** and is used for masculine and feminine plural.

AUDIO 17.1 📢

CES – *These/those*

Use **ces** before a plural noun.

> **Ces téléphones** – *These/Those phones*
> **Ces oranges** – *These/Those oranges*

In chapter 16, we saw that **ses** is a possessive adjective meanings *his/her/its*. It's the plural of **son** and **sa** and is used for masculine and feminine plural, just like **ces**.

AUDIO 17.2 📢

SES – *His/her/its*

Use **ses** before a plural noun.

> **Ses téléphones** – *His/her phones*
> **Ses oranges** – *His/her oranges*

AUDIO 17.3 📢

 Ajoutez **ces** ou **ses** aux phrases suivantes. Regardez à la traduction pour vous aider.
Add ces or ses to the following sentences. Look to the translation to help you.

1. Qui a peint _____ peintures ?
   Who painted these paintings?

2. _____ enfants ne regardent jamais la télévision.
   Her children never watch television.

3. Est-ce que tu as vu   articles dans le journal ?

Have you seen these articles in the newspaper?

4. Qu'est-ce que vous pensez de   idées ?

What do you think of his ideas?

5. Est-ce que tu veux goûter un de   macarons ?

Do you want to try one of these macaroons?

6. Qu'est-ce que   personnes sont devenues ?

What happened to these people?

7.   chaussures sont des chaussures de marque.

His shoes are designer shoes.

8. Tu as pensé à appeler   clients ?

Have you thought about calling these customers?

9. Elle a encadré   photos préférées.

She framed her favorite photos.

10.   maisons ont été rénovées récemment.

These houses have been recently renovated.

11.   lunettes sont à elle.

These glasses are hers.

12.   nouveaux meubles sont plus modernes que les anciens.

His new furniture is more modern than the old ones.

13. Il a accueilli   premiers clients ce matin.

He welcomed his first customers this morning.

14. Quel est le nom de   montagnes ?

What are the names of these mountains?

15. Il perd toujours   affaires !

He always loses his things!

NOTRE NOTRE NOS – VOTRE VOTRE VOS – LEUR LEUR LEURS

18

OUR – YOUR – THEIR

In chapter 16, we looked at singular French possessive adjectives. Now, let's look at the plural ones.

> **Notre notre nos** *(our)*, **votre votre vos** *(your)*, **leur leur leurs** *(their)* are French possessive adjectives. They are used the same way as in English. They can be followed by a noun or an adjective. They are easier than the singular ones because they don't change with gender. They are the same for feminine or masculine.

	Masucline	Feminine	Plural
Our	notre	notre	nos
Your	votre	votre	vos
Their	leur	leur	leurs

AUDIO 18.1 ◄))

NOTRE – NOTRE – NOS – *Our*

Notre ordinateur est lent. *Our computer is slow.*
Notre voiture est neuve. *Our car is new.*
Nos lettres sont arrivées. *Our letters have arrived.*

VOTRE – VOTRE – VOS – *Your*

Votre ordinateur est lent. *Your computer is slow.*
Votre voiture est neuve. *Your car is new.*
Vos lettres sont arrivées. *Your letters have arrived.*

LEUR – LEUR – LEURS – *Their*

Leur ordinateur est lent. *Their computer is slow.*
Leur voiture est neuve. *Their car is new.*
Leurs lettres sont arrivées. *Their letters have arrived.*

Ajoutez **notre notre nos** – **votre votre vos** – **leur leur leurs** à chaque phrase.
Regardez à la traduction pour vous aider.
Add notre notre nos – votre votre vos – leur leur leurs to each sentence. Look to the translation to help you.

1. _____ amis viennent nous rendre visite ce soir.
   Our friends are coming to visit us tonight.

2. _____ chiens n'obéissent pas beaucoup.
   Your dogs don't obey much.

3. _____ enfants vont à l'école ensemble.
   Our children go to school together.

4. _____ anniversaire de mariage est le même jour que le nôtre.
   Their wedding anniversary is the same day as ours.

5. _____ maison est située à une centaine de mètres de la plage.
   Our house is located about a hundred meters from the beach.

6. _____ jardin est plein de fleurs.
   Their garden is full of flowers.

7. Bien sûr que _____ avis est important pour nous.
   Of course, your opinion is important to us.

8. _____ nouvelle cuisine est équipée des derniers gadgets.
   Their new kitchen is equipped with the latest gadgets.

9. _____ projet de construction avance bien.
   Our construction project is progressing well.

10. _____ rendez-vous sont prévus pour demain matin.
    Your appointments are scheduled for tomorrow morning.

11. _____ nouvel appartement est beaucoup plus spacieux.
    Our new apartment is much more spacious.

12. _____ chat se promène souvent dans le quartier.

Their cat often wanders around the neighborhood.

13. _____ voyage en Europe est réservé pour le mois prochain.

Our trip to Europe is booked for next month.

14. Est-ce que _____ nouvelle voiture est une voiture électrique ?

Is your new car an electric car?

15. _____ voisins organisent toujours un barbecue en été.

Our neighbors always organize a barbecue in the summer.

LES NOMBRES
NUMBERS

19

Let's learn or review French numbers!

AUDIO 19.1 ◀))

1 **Un - Une** – *One*	15 **Quinze** – *Fifteen*
2 **Deux** – *Two*	16 **Seize** – *Sixteen*
3 **Trois** – *Three*	17 **Dix-sept** – *Seventeen*
4 **Quatre** – *Four*	18 **Dix-huit** – *Eighteen*
5 **Cinq** – *Five*	19 **Dix-neuf** – *Nineteen*
6 **Six** – *Six*	20 **Vingt** – *Twenty*
7 **Sept** – *Seven*	30 **Trente** – *Thirty*
8 **Huit** – *Eight*	40 **Quarante** – *Forty*
9 **Neuf** – *Nine*	50 **Cinquante** – *Fifty*
10 **Dix** – *Ten*	60 **Soixante** – *Sixty*
11 **Onze** – *Eleven*	70 **Soixante-dix** – *Seventy*
12 **Douze** – *Twelve*	80 **Quatre-vingts** – *Eighty*
13 **Treize** – *Thirteen*	90 **Quatre-vingt-dix** – *Ninety*
14 **Quatorze** – *Fourteen*	100 **Cent** – *One hundred*

From **21 to 69**, all numbers follow the same pattern:

AUDIO 19.2 ◀))

21 **Vingt et un** – *Twenty-one*	26 **Vingt-six** – *Twenty-six*
22 **Vingt-deux** – *Twenty-two*	27 **Vingt-sept** – *Twenty-seven*
23 **Vingt-trois** – *Twenty-three*	28 **Vingt-huit** – *Twenty-eight*
24 **Vingt-quatre** – *Twenty-four*	29 **Vingt-neuf** – *Twenty-nine*
25 **Vingt-cinq** – *Twenty-five*	

70 = 60 + 10

70 **Soixante-dix** – *Seventy*	75 **Soixante-quinze** – *Seventy-five*
71 **Soixante et onze** – *Seventy-one*	76 **Soixante-seize** – *Seventy-six*
72 **Soixante-douze** – *Seventy-two*	77 **Soixante-dix-sept** – *Seventy-seven*
73 **Soixante-treize** – *Seventy-three*	78 **Soixante-dix-huit** – *Seventy-eight*
74 **Soixante-quatorze** – *Seventy-four*	79 **Soixante-dix-neuf** – *Seventy-nine*

80 = 4 x 20

80 **Quatre-vingts** – *Eighty*	85 **Quatre-vingt-cinq** – *Eighty-five*
81 **Quatre-vingt-un** – *Eighty-one*	86 **Quatre-vingt-six** – *Eighty-six*
82 **Quatre-vingt-deux** – *Eighty-two*	87 **Quatre-vingt-sept** – *Eighty-seven*
83 **Quatre-vingt-trois** – *Eighty-three*	88 **Quatre-vingt-huit** – *Eighty-eight*
84 **Quatre-vingt-quatre** – *Eighty-four*	89 **Quatre-vingt-neuf** – *Eighty-nine*

90 = 4 x 20 + 10

90 **Quatre-vingt-dix** – *Ninety*	95 **Quatre-vingt-quinze** – *Ninety-five*
91 **Quatre-vingt-onze** – *Ninety-one*	96 **Quatre-vingt-seize** – *Ninety-six*
92 **Quatre-vingt-douze** – *Ninety-two*	97 **Quatre-vingt-dix-sept** – *Ninety-seven*
93 **Quatre-vingt-treize** – *Ninety-three*	98 **Quatre-vingt-dix-huit** – *Ninety-eight*
94 **Quatre-vingt-quatorze** – *Ninety-four*	99 **Quatre-vingt-dix-neuf** – *Ninety-nine*

AUDIO 19.3 🔊

 Écrivez les nombres en lettres.
Write the numbers in letters.

11 –

19 –

21 –

29 –

36 –

47 –

52 –

63 –

72 –

77 –

80 –

89 –

92 –

99 –

100 –

LA NÉGATION SIMPLE
SIMPLE NEGATION

Simple negation *(not)* is made of two words in French: **ne** and **pas**.
Ne will be shortened to **n'** when the verb starts with a vowel or a silent h.

AUDIO 20.1 🔊

ne/n' + verb + pas

> **Je mange.** *I am eating.*
> **Je ne mange pas.** *I am not eating.*

When the verb is conjugated in **passé composé** or other **compound tenses**, the negation is placed around the auxiliary and is followed by the past participle.

ne/n' + auxiliary + pas + past participle

> **J'ai mangé.** *I ate.*
> **Je n'ai pas mangé.** *I didn't eat.*

When pas is followed by an indefinite article « **un – une – des** » or a partitive article « **du – de la – de l' – des** », any of these articles become **de**. **De** becomes **d'** before a word starting with a vowel or a silent h.

ne + verb + pas + de/d'

> **Il mange une pomme.** *He is eating an apple.*
> **Il ne mange pas de pomme.** *He is not eating an apple.*

AUDIO 20.2 🔊

 Transformez **les phrases affirmatives** en **phrases négatives** avec **ne ... pas**.
Change the sentences from affirmative to negative with ne ... pas.

1. J'ai le temps de prendre un café.
   I have time for coffee.

---

2. Tu es en retard.
   You are late.

3. Vous voulez venir avec nous ?
   Do you want to come with us?

4. Elle lit quelques chapitres avant de dormir.
   She reads a few chapters before sleeping.

5. Mon père regarde les informations tous les soirs.
   My father watches the news every night.

6. J'ai un chien qui s'appelle Max.
   I have a dog named Max.

7. Elle sera là samedi.
   She will be there on Saturday.

8. J'ai bien compris la question.
   I understood the question correctly.

9. On a acheté une petite maison dans le sud de la France.
   We bought a small house in the south of France.

10. Il a fait des efforts ces derniers mois.
    He's made an effort these last few months.

11. Je porte des chaussures.
    I am wearing shoes.

12. Il fait beau ce matin.

The weather is nice this morning.

13. Il manque une pièce dans ce jeu de société.

There is a piece missing in this board game.

14. J'ai vu mon patron au parc.

I saw my boss at the park.

15. Elle aime la musique classique.

She likes classical music.

PASSÉ COMPOSÉ – ÊTRE OU AVOIR ?
PASSÉ COMPOSÉ – ÊTRE OR AVOIR?

The **passé composé** is a past compound tense made of the auxiliary **avoir** *(to have)* or *être (to be)* conjugated in the **présent** followed by a **participe passé**.

Subject + avoir/être + participe passé

We have seen the conjugation of **être** and **avoir** in the present tense in chapters 6 and 14 but let's review them one more time!

Avoir – *To have*

AUDIO 21.1 ◀))

J'ai – *I have*
Tu as – *You have*
Il a – *He has*
Elle a – *She has*
On a – *We have*
Nous avons – *We have*
Vous avez – *You have*
Ils ont – *They have (m)*
Elles ont – *They have (f)*

Être – *To be*

AUDIO 21.2 ◀))

Je suis – *I am*
Tu es – *You are*
Il est – *He is*
Elle est – *She is*
On est – *We are*
Nous sommes – *We are*
Vous êtes – *You are*
Ils sont – *They are (m)*
Elles sont – *They are (f)*

Most verbs in French are conjugated with the auxiliary **avoir**.

A list of specific verbs, as well as all reflexive verbs, are conjugated in the **passé composé** with the auxiliary **être**. To remember them, remember the rule of **DR & MRS VANDERTRAMPP**, each letter corresponding to a verb conjugated with **être**.

AUDIO 21.3 ◀))

Infinitive	Translation	Past participle
Devenir	*To become*	**Devenu**
Revenir	*To come back*	**Revenu**
&		
Monter	*To go up*	**Monté**
Rester	*To stay*	**Resté**
Sortir	*To go out*	**Sorti**

Venir	*To come*	**Venu**
Aller	*To go*	**Allé**
Naître	*To be born*	**Né**
Descendre	*To go down*	**Descendu**
Entrer	*To enter*	**Entré**
Rentrer	*To go home*	**Rentré**
Tomber	*To fall*	**Tombé**
Retourner	*To return*	**Retourné**
Arriver	*To arrive*	**Arrivé**
Mourir	*To die*	**Mort**
Partir	*To leave*	**Parti**
Passer	*To pass by*	**Passé**

AUDIO 21.4 ◄))

Ajoutez l'auxiliaire **avoir** ou **être** conjugué au **présent** avant chaque **participe passé**. Ajoutez aussi l'infinitif du verbe entre parenthèses si vous le connaissez.
Add the auxiliary avoir or être conjugated in the present tense before each past participle. Also, add the infinitive of the verb in parentheses if you know it.

1. Il _____ **monté** dans l'ascenseur après moi. (_____)
   He got in the elevator after me.

2. On _____ **mangé** des pâtes pour le déjeuner. (_____)
   We had pasta for lunch.

3. Est-ce que tu _____ **vu** ce film ? (_____)
   Have you seen this movie?

4. Il _____ **parti** il y a deux heures. (_____)
   He left two hours ago.

5. Elle _____ **pris** les décisions pour la réunion. (_____)
   She made the decisions for the meeting.

6. Ma fille _____ **commencé** à marcher tard. (_____)
   My daughter started walking late.

7. La caissière _____ **oublié** de me donner le ticket. (_____)
   The cashier forgot to give me the receipt.

8. Il _____ **plu** hier. ( )

It rained yesterday.

9. Mes parents _____ **venus** manger à la maison. ( )

My parents came to eat at home.

10. Ils **se** _____ **mariés** le mois dernier. ( )

They got married last month.

11. J' _____ **bu** un café délicieux. ( )

I drank a delicious coffee.

12. Elle _____ **agi** sans réfléchir. ( )

She acted without thinking.

13. Les ambulanciers _____ **arrivés** tout de suite. ( )

The paramedics arrived straight away.

14. Est-ce qu'ils _____ **vendu** leur voiture ? ( )

Did they sell their car?

15. Les enfants _____ **fait** leurs devoirs dans le salon. ( )

The children did their homework in the living room.

LE PARTICIPE PASSÉ DES VERBES
THE PAST PARTICIPLE OF VERBS

22

The **past participle of verbs** changes depending on the group of verbs and whether the verb is regular or irregular. We can find the same in English with regulars: *searched, painted, called*, and irregulars: *ate, brought*, etc.

AUDIO 22.1 ◄))

Regular verbs in French are divided into 3 groups:

- 1st group **-er** verbs change from the ending **er** to the ending **é**

    Manger - mangé   *To eat - ate*

- 2nd group **-ir** verbs change from the ending **ir** to the ending **i**

    Finir - fini   *To finish - finished*

- 3rd group **-re** verbs change from the ending **re** to the ending **u**

    Attendre - attendu   *To wait - waited*

AUDIO 22.2 ◄))

And of course, we have common irregular past participles:

Avoir - eu	*To have - had*
Boire - bu	*To drink - drank*
Conduire - conduit	*To drive - driven*
Connaître - connu	*To know - known*
Devoir - dû	*To have to - had to*
Être - été	*To be - been*
Lire - lu	*To read - read*
Mettre - mis	*To put - put*
Pouvoir - pu	*To be able - been able*
Recevoir - reçu	*To recieve - recieved*
Savoir - su	*To know - known*
Tenir - tenu	*To hold - held*
Venir - venu	*To come - came*
Vouloir - voulu	*To want - wanted*

> Ajoutez **le participe passé** du verbe entre parenthèses. Quand le verbe est conjugué avec **être**, accordez-le au sujet de la phrase si besoin.
> *Add the past participle of the verb in parentheses. When conjugated with être, match it to the subject of the sentence if necessary.*

1. Ils sont _____ à la maison toute la journée. (**rester**)
   They stayed at home all day.

2. La chanteuse a _____ l'hymne national. (**chanter**)
   The singer sang the national anthem.

3. Est-ce que tu as bien _____ ? (**dormir**)
   Did you sleep well?

4. Le coureur a _____ pour finir la course. (**marcher**)
   The runner walked to finish the race.

5. J'ai _____ quelque chose de bizarre. (**entendre**)
   I heard something strange.

6. Il a _____ ses enfants à l'aéroport. (**conduire**)
   He drove his children to the airport.

7. On a _____ un chien au refuge. (**adopter**)
   We adopted a dog from the shelter.

8. J'ai _____ ce livre mais je ne l'ai pas _____. (**lire - aimer**)
   I read this book, but I didn't like it.

9. Il n'est pas _____ avec moi. (**venir**)
   He didn't come with me.

10. Elles se sont _____ ensemble ce matin. (**se préparer**)
    They got ready together this morning.

11. Le technicien a _____ le filtre. (**remplacer**)
    The technician replaced the filter.

12. Mon voisin a _____ mon colis par erreur. (**recevoir**)

My neighbor received my package by mistake.

13. Elle a _____ ses mémoires il y a quelques années. (**écrire**)

She wrote her memoirs a few years ago.

14. Qu'est-ce que tu as _____ ? (**choisir**)

What did you choose?

15. On t'a _____ toute la soirée. (**attendre**)

We waited for you all evening.

LE PARTICIPE PASSÉ ET L'INFINITIF

PAST PARTICIPLE AND INFINITIVE

23

French verbs can be conjugated or not. When they are not conjugated, they are called *infinitive* – **infinitif**. In English, an infinitive verb starts with *to*: *To eat* – *To sleep* – *To learn* - ... In French, infinitive verbs keep their endings: **manger** – **dormir** – **apprendre** - ...

French use infinitive verbs more than English.

In this exercise, we are going to learn when to use the past participle or the infinitive.

When to Use a Past Participle?

AUDIO 23.1 ◀))

The past participle of French verbs is mostly used in compound tenses after the auxiliary **avoir** or **être**.

J'ai <u>mangé</u> une pomme. *I ate an apple.*
→ The past participle is **mangé** from the infinitive verb **manger**.

Il a <u>dormi</u> toute la journée. *He slept all day.*
→ The past participle is **dormi** from the infinitive verb **dormir**.

Elle a <u>appris</u> sa leçon. *She learned her lesson.*
→ The past participle is **appris** from the infinitive verb **apprendre**.

When to Use an Infinitive Verb?

AUDIO 23.2 ◀))

We use infinitive verbs in 4 different sentence structures in French.

- After the preposition **à**

  J'ai réussi à <u>dormir</u>. *I was able to sleep.*

- After the preposition **de**

  Le chien a envie de <u>jouer</u>. *The dog wants to play.*

- After the preposition **pour**

  Il a acheté un cahier pour <u>prendre</u> des notes. *He bought a notebook to take notes.*

– As a second verb (this is different than a compound tense). The first verb can be conjugated in any tense.

Je veux <u>chanter</u> cette chanson. *I want to sing this song.*

 Dans les phrases ci-dessous, est-ce qu'il manque **le participe passé** ou **le verbe infinitif** ? Choisissez entre les deux. Le premier est **le participe passé**. Le deuxième est **le verbe infinitif**.
In the sentences below, is the past participle or infinitive verb missing? Choose between the two. The first is the past participle. The second is the infinitive verb.

1. Le chien veut _____ à la balle.
   (joué / jouer)
   The dog wants to play with the ball.

2. Elle adore _____ .
   (dansé / danser)
   She loves to dance.

3. Qu'est-ce que tu as _____ ?
   (fait / faire)
   What did you do?

4. J'ai _____ de nouveaux produits pour _____ .
   (acheté / acheter – nettoyé / nettoyer)
   I bought new products for cleaning.

5. Est-ce que tu as _____ ton examen ?
   (réussi / réussir)
   Did you pass your exam?

6. Il n'a pas _____ à _____ la police.
   (pensé / penser – appelé / appeler)
   He didn't think to call the police.

7. Je n'arrive pas à y _____ .
   (cru / croire)
   I can't believe it.

8. Elle a _____ des fleurs à sa mère.
    (offert / offrir)

    She offered flowers to her mother.

9. Les enfants ont _____ à _____ à l'école.
    (appris / apprendre – compté / compter)

    The children learned to count at school.

10. Elle a _____ la lumière avant de _____ .
    (éteint / éteindre – sorti / sortir)

    She turned off the light before leaving.

11. Je n'ai pas _____ avec toi.
    (pu / pouvoir – venu / venir)

    I couldn't come with you.

12. Ça m'a beaucoup _____ .
    (fait / faire – ri / rire)

    That made me laugh a lot.

13. Qu'est-ce qu'il est _____ ?
    (devenu / devenir)

    What did he become?

14. On a _____ nos premiers clients.
    (accueilli / accueillir)

    We welcomed our first customers.

15. Est-ce que vous avez _____ à _____ de voiture ?
    (réfléchi / réfléchir – changé / changer)

    Have you considered changing cars?

TROUVEZ LES ERREURS

FIND THE ERRORS

24

Time for a recap! Here are 15 questions related to everything we have seen from chapter 8 to the last chapter. Each answer is explained in the solutions.

AUDIO 24.1 ◀))

 Trouvez **les erreurs** dans les phrases ci-dessous.
Find the errors in the sentences below.

1. J'ai lu tous les livres de ce auteur.
   I have read all of this author's books.

2. Sa amie va passer le week-end chez nous.
   Her friend is going to spend the weekend with us.

3. Leur chiens jouent au parc pendant qu'ils discutent.
   Their dogs play at the park while they talk.

4. Il n'est jamais de chance !
   He is never lucky!

5. À quelle heure est-ce que tu réveilles ?
   What time do you wake up?

6. Les manteau que j'ai commandé n'est pas encore arrivé.
   The coat I ordered hasn't arrived yet.

7. Quel âge est-ce que tu vas a ?
How old are you going to be?

8. Je sèche les mains.
I am drying my hands.

9. Est-ce que tu t'es brossé tes cheveux ?
Did you brush your hair?

10. On avais toujours du beau temps en été.
We always had good weather in summer.

11. Mon grand-père a soixante dix-neuf ans.
My grandfather is seventy-nine years old.

12. Je n'ai pas fait une faute dans mon examen.
I didn't make a mistake in my exam.

13. Il a tombé en faisant du vélo.
He fell while riding his bike.

14. Tu n'as toujours pas recevu la lettre que je t'ai envoyée ?
You still haven't received the letter I sent you?

15. N'oublie pas de débranché le fer à repasser quand tu as fini.
Don't forget to unplug the iron when you're finished.

LA PRÉPOSITION À

THE PREPOSITION À

The preposition **à** can be found as **à** or as **au** – **aux** – **à la** – **à l'** when followed by a noun.
À can also be followed by a verb, we will see it in chapter 27.

The Different Forms of the Preposition à

AUDIO 25.1 ◄))

à + le = **au** + singular masculine noun

au dentiste – *to the dentist*

à + les = **aux** + plural masculine or feminine noun

aux enfants – *to the children*

à + la = **à la** + singular feminine noun

à la caissière – *to the cashier*

à + l' = **à l'** + singular masculine or feminine noun starting with a vowel or a silent h

à l'employé – *to the employee (m)*
à l'employée – *to the employee (f)*

20 Common Verbs Followed by à and a Noun

AUDIO 25.2 ◄))

Verb + à + noun

Aller à quelqu'un	*To suit somebody*
Croire à quelque chose	*To believe something*
Demander à quelqu'un	*To ask somebody*
Dire à quelqu'un	*To say to somebody - To tell somebody*
Donner à quelqu'un	*To give to somebody*
Écrire à quelqu'un	*To write to somebody*
Faire attention à quelqu'un - quelque chose	*To pay attention to somebody - something*
Faire confiance à quelqu'un	*To trust somebody*
Faire mal à quelqu'un	*To hurt somebody*
Jouer à quelque chose	*To play something*
Pardonner à quelqu'un	*To forgive somebody*

Parler à quelqu'un	*To talk to somebody*
Penser à quelqu'un – quelque chose	*To think about somebody - something*
Réfléchir à quelque chose	*To consider - reflect upon something*
Rendre visite à quelqu'un	*To visit somebody*
Répondre à quelqu'un	*To answer somebody*
S'habituer à quelqu'un	*To get used to somebody*
S'intéresser à quelqu'un - quelque chose	*To be interested by somebody - something*
Sourire à quelqu'un	*To smile to somebody*
Téléphoner à quelqu'un	*To call somebody*

AUDIO 25.3

Ajoutez la préposition **à – au – aux – à la – à l'**, à chaque phrase.
Add the preposition à – au – aux – à la – à l', to each sentence.

1. Elle a pardonné   voleurs.
   She forgave the thieves.

2. Fais attention   marche.
   Watch your step.

3. Je ne fais pas confiance   personnes que je ne connais pas.
   I don't trust people I don't know.

4. On s'intéresse   plantes de notre jardin.
   We are interested in the plants in our garden.

5. Elle a dit   coiffeur de couper ses cheveux courts.
   She told the hairdresser to cut her hair short.

6. Je dois répondre   message de mon frère.
   I need to respond to my brother's message.

7. Tu veux jouer   cartes avec nous ?
   Do you want to play cards with us?

8. Ce sac va très bien   mannequin.
   This bag suits the model very well.

9. Le docteur rend visite _____ patients tous les matins.

    The doctor visits the patients every morning.

10. On a téléphoné _____ mairie mais personne n'a répondu.

    We called city hall but no one answered.

11. Elle a donné son ticket _____ homme devant elle.

    She gave her ticket to the man in front of her.

12. Il ne croit pas _____ Père Noël.

    He doesn't believe in Santa Claus.

13. Je m'habitue _____ températures assez vite.

    I get used to temperatures quite quickly.

14. Est-ce que tu as parlé _____ architecte ?

    Did you talk to the architect?

15. J'écris une lettre _____ docteurs.

    I am writing a letter to the doctors.

LA PRÉPOSITION DE

THE PREPOSITION DE

26

Just like the preposition **à**, the preposition **de** will take different forms when followed by a noun. It can change to **du – des – de la – de l'**. **De** can also be followed by a verb, we will see it in chapter 27.

The Different Forms of the Preposition de

AUDIO 26.1 ◄))

de + le = du + singular masculine noun

du téléphone – *phone*

de + les = des + plural masculine or feminine noun

des araignées – *spiders*

de + la = de la + singular feminine noun

de la voiture – *car*

de + l' = de l' + singular masculine or feminine noun starting with a vowel or a silent h

de l'aéroport – *airport*
de l'école – *school*

20 Common Verbs Followed by de and a Noun

AUDIO 26.2 ◄))

Verb + de + noun

Arriver de + endroit	*To arrive from + place*
Avoir besoin de quelqu'un - quelque chose	*To need somebody - something*
Avoir envie de quelque chose	*To want something*
Avoir peur de quelqu'un - quelque chose	*To be afraid of somebody - something*
Dépendre de quelqu'un - quelque chose	*To depend on somebody - something*
Hériter de quelque chose	*To inherit something*
Parler de quelqu'un - quelque chose	*To talk about somebody - something*
Partir de + endroit	*To leave + place*
Penser de quelqu'un - quelque chose	*To think of somebody - something*
Profiter de quelqu'un - quelque chose	*To take advantage of somebody - something*

Rêver de quelqu'un - quelque chose	*To dream of somebody - something*
Rire de quelqu'un - quelque chose	*To laugh at somebody - something*
S'agir de quelqu'un - quelque chose	*To be about somebody - something*
S'occuper de quelqu'un - quelque chose	*To take care of somebody - something*
Se méfier de quelqu'un	*To mistrust somebody*
Se moquer de quelqu'un	*To make fun of somebody*
Se passer de quelqu'un - quelque chose	*To do without somebody - something*
Se plaindre de quelqu'un - quelque chose	*To complain about somebody - something*
Se servir de quelqu'un - quelque chose	*To use somebody - something*
Se souvenir de quelqu'un - quelque chose	*To remember somebody - something*

 AUDIO 26.3 ◀))

Ajoutez la préposition **de – du – des – de la – de l'**, à chaque phrase.
Add the preposition de – du – des – de la – de l', to each sentence.

1. Il a toujours eu peur   serpents.
He was always afraid of snakes.

2. On vient juste de partir   aéroport.
We just left the airport.

3. J'ai envie   chocolat que j'ai acheté hier.
I'm craving the chocolate I bought yesterday.

4. Méfie-toi   voisins.
Beware of the neighbors.

5. Elle a hérité   maison de ses parents.
She inherited her parents' house.

6. Il a profité   problème.
He took advantage of the problem.

7. Je me sers   friteuse de temps en temps.
I use the fryer from time to time.

8. Qu'est-ce que tu penses   film ?
What do you think of the movie?

9. Tu te souviens _____ personne qui conduisait ?

Do you remember who was driving?

10. Il s'agit _____ papier que j'ai perdu.

This is the paper I lost.

11. Les spectateurs rient _____ blague.

The spectators are laughing at the joke.

12. Tu leur as parlé _____ vacances ?

Did you tell them about the holidays?

13. On a besoin _____ journal que je t'ai donné hier.

We need the newspaper I gave you yesterday.

14. Les invités arrivent _____ mariage.

The guests are arriving from the wedding.

15. Elle se plaint toujours _____ température.

She always complains about the temperature.

LES PRÉPOSITIONS À ET DE

PREPOSITIONS À AND DE

27

The prepositions **à** and **de** can be followed by a noun (as we saw in chapters 25 and 26) or an infinitive verb. In this exercise, we will focus on the prepositions **à** and **de** followed by an infinitive verb.

à + infinitive verb

de + infinitive verb

French verbs and their prepositions should be learned by heart, as there is no rule to know which preposition goes with each verb.

Last, the preposition always goes <u>with the verb before the preposition</u>, not the verb after.

20 Common Verbs Followed by à and an Infinitive Verb

AUDIO 27.1 ◀))

Verb + à + infinitive verb

Aider à faire quelque chose	*To help to do something*
Apprendre à faire quelque chose	*To learn how to do something*
Arriver à faire quelque chose	*To be able to do something*
Avoir à faire quelque chose	*To have to do something*
Chercher à faire quelque chose	*To attempt to do something*
Commencer à faire quelque chose	*To begin to do something*
Continuer à faire quelque chose	*To continue to do something*
Hésiter à faire quelque chose	*To hesitate to do something*
Parvenir à faire quelque chose	*To succeed in doing something*
Passer du temps à faire quelque chose	*To spend time doing something*
Penser à faire quelque chose	*To think about doing something*
Réfléchir à faire quelque chose	*To think of doing something*
Renoncer à faire quelque chose	*To give up on doing something*
Réussir à faire quelque chose	*To succeed in doing something*
S'engager à faire quelque chose	*To commit to something*
S'habituer à faire quelque chose	*To get used to do something*
Se consacrer à faire quelque chose	*To devote yourself to doing something*
Se mettre à faire quelque chose	*To start doing something*
Songer à faire quelque chose	*To think about doing something*
Tenir à faire quelque chose	*To insist on doing something*

Il a réussi <u>à</u> changer le lustre du salon. *He managed to change the chandelier in the living room.*

Common Verbs Followed by de and an Infinitive Verb

AUDIO 27.2 🔊

Verb + de + infinitive verb

Accepter de faire quelque chose	*To accept to do something*
Arrêter de faire quelque chose	*To stop doing something*
Avoir besoin de faire quelque chose	*To need to do something*
Avoir envie de faire quelque chose	*To feel like doing something*
Avoir peur de faire quelque chose	*To be afraid of doing something*
Avoir raison de faire quelque chose	*To be right to do something*
Avoir tort de faire quelque chose	*To be wrong to do something*
Choisir de faire quelque chose	*To choose to do something*
Continuer de faire quelque chose	*To keep doing something*
Décider de faire quelque chose	*To decide to do something*
Essayer de faire quelque chose	*To try to do something*
Être en train de faire quelque chose	*To be in the process of doing something*
Être sur le point de faire quelque chose	*To be about to do something*
Finir de faire quelque chose	*To finish doing something*
Oublier de faire quelque chose	*To forget to do something*
Parler de faire quelque chose	*To talk about doing something*
Refuser de faire quelque chose	*To refuse to do something*
Rêver de faire quelque chose	*To dream of doing something*
Se souvenir de faire quelque chose	*To remember doing something*
Venir de faire quelque chose	*To have just done something*
	(Passé récent – recent past)

Il a choisi <u>de</u> revenir plus tôt de son voyage. *He chose to return early from his trip.*

AUDIO 27.3 🔊

 Ajoutez la préposition **à** ou **de/d'** après chaque verbe.
Add the preposition à or de/d' after each verb.

1. Il a choisi   vendre son entreprise l'année dernière.
   He chose to sell his business last year.

2. Est-ce que tu peux m'aider   préparer le repas ?
   Can you help me prepare the meal?

3. Mon fils rêve   devenir astronaute.
   My son dreams of becoming an astronaut.

4. J'ai appris   jouer de la guitare quand j'étais petite.

 I learned to play the guitar when I was little.

5. Il a peur   se faire mal.

 He is afraid of getting hurt.

6. On hésite   réserver nos vacances maintenant.

 We are hesitating to book our vacation now.

7. Elles sont sur le point   partir.

 They are about to leave.

8. Le directeur tient   remercier tous ses employés.

 The director would like to thank all his employees.

9. N'oublie pas   te brosser les dents.

 Don't forget to brush your teeth.

10. Il cherche   réussir sans travailler.

 He tries to succeed without working.

11. Elle a accepté   m'aider ce samedi.

 She agreed to help me this Saturday.

12. Est-ce que tu continues   étudier pendant les vacances ?

 Do you continue to study during the holidays?

13. On vient   partir.

 We just left.

14. J'ai réussi   arrêter   fumer.

 I managed to quit smoking.

15. Tu devrais essayer   travailler un peu plus.

 You should try to work a little more.

ALLER SUIVI D'UN PAYS
ALLER FOLLOWED BY A COUNTRY

28

Aller is, of course, used as a verb of motion: *To go somewhere.*

It's always followed by a preposition, including when followed by a country. The preposition will change depending on the gender of the country. In French, countries are either <u>masculine</u>, <u>feminine</u>, or <u>plural</u>.

Most countries in French ending with **-e** are feminine, besides **Le Mexique** *(Mexico)*. Countries ending with **-s** are plural, and the rest are masculine.

AUDIO 28.1 ◀))

Aller + en

Use **en** when followed by a feminine country or when a country starts with a vowel, either masculine or feminine.

Aller en Belgique	*To go to Belgium*
Aller en Iran	*To go to Iran*

Aller + au

Use **au** when followed by a masculine country starting with a consonant.

Aller au Canada	*To go to Canada*
Aller au Portugal	*To go to Portugal*

Aller + aux

Use **aux** when followed by a plural country.

Aller aux États-Unis	*To go to the United States*
Aller aux Pays-Bas	*To go to the Netherlands*

AUDIO 28.2 ◀))

 Ajoutez la préposition **au, aux** ou **en** avant chaque pays.
Add the preposition au, aux, or en before each country.

1.	Aller	Koweït	*To go to Kuwait*
2.	Aller	Italie	*To go to Italy*

3.	Aller	Canada	*To go to Canada*
4.	Aller	Vietnam	*To go to Vietnam*
5.	Aller	Irak	*To go to Iraq*
6.	Aller	Égypte	*To go to Egypt*
7.	Aller	Ghana	*To go to Ghana*
8.	Aller	Chine	*To go to China*
9.	Aller	Royaume-Uni	*To go to the UK*
10.	Aller	Inde	*To go to India*
11.	Aller	Sri Lanka	*To go to Sri Lanka*
12.	Aller	Thaïlande	*To go to Thailand*
13.	Aller	Iran	*To go to Iran*
14.	Aller	Tanzanie	*To go to Tanzania*
15.	Aller	Qatar	*To go to Qatar*
16.	Aller	Espagne	*To go to Spain*
17.	Aller	Liban	*To go to Lebanon*
18.	Aller	Argentine	*To go to Argentina*
19.	Aller	Kenya	*To go to Kenya*
20.	Aller	Pérou	*To go to Peru*
21.	Aller	Turquie	*To go to Türkiye*
22.	Aller	Philippines	*To go to the Philippines*
23.	Aller	Afrique du Sud	*To go to South Africa*
24.	Aller	Nigéria	*To go to Nigeria*
25.	Aller	Japon	*To go to Japan*
26.	Aller	Australie	*To go to Australia*
27.	Aller	Mexique	*To go to Mexico*
28.	Aller	Colombie	*To go to Colombia*
29.	Aller	États-Unis	*To go to the United States*
30.	Aller	Indonésie	*To go to Indonesia*
31.	Aller	Brésil	*To go to Brazil*
32.	Aller	Jordanie	*To go to Jordan*
33.	Aller	Malaisie	*To go to Malaysia*
34.	Aller	Bangladesh	*To go to Bangladesh*

35.	Aller	Arabie Saoudite	*To go to Saudi Arabia*
36.	Aller	Pakistan	*To go to Pakistan*
37.	Aller	Syrie	*To go to Syria*
38.	Aller	France	*To go to France*
39.	Aller	Allemagne	*To go to Germany*
40.	Aller	Afghanistan	*To go to Afghanistan*

LA CONJUGAISON DE FAIRE

THE CONJUGATION OF FAIRE

29

The verb **faire** is probably the most versatile verb in French. We use it to talk about what we do, make, play, bake, to talk about the weather, and more! Its conjugation is irregular so let's learn or review it before practicing. Try to remember its conjugation by heart.

Faire translates to *To do/To make* but in the following conjugation, I am only going to translate to *To do* so it's easier. In the exercise, you will see that the translation of **faire** doesn't always match in English.

Présent de l'indicatif

AUDIO 29.1 ◄))

Je fais – *I do*
Tu fais – *You do*
Il-Elle fait – *He-She does*
On fait – *We do*
Nous faisons – *We do*
Vous faites – *You do*
Ils-Elles font – *They do*

Imparfait

AUDIO 29.3 ◄))

Je faisais – *I did*
Tu faisais – *You did*
Il-Elle faisait – *He-She did*
On faisait – *We did*
Nous faisions – *We did*
Vous faisiez – *You did*
Ils-Elles faisaient – *They did*

Conditionnel présent

AUDIO 29.5 ◄))

Je ferais – *I would do*
Tu ferais – *You would do*
Il-Elle ferait – *He-She would do*
On ferait – *We would do*
Nous ferions – *We would do*
Vous feriez – *You would do*
Ils-Elles feraient – *They would do*

Passé composé

AUDIO 29.2 ◄))

J'ai fait – *I did*
Tu as fait – *You did*
Il-Elle a fait – *He-She did*
On a fait – *We did*
Nous avons fait – *We did*
Vous avez fait – *You did*
Ils-Elles ont fait – *They did*

Futur simple

AUDIO 29.4 ◄))

Je ferai – *I will do*
Tu feras – *You will do*
Il-Elle fera – *He-She will do*
On fera – *We will do*
Nous ferons – *We will do*
Vous ferez – *You will do*
Ils-Elles feront – *They will do*

Subjonctif présent

AUDIO 29.6 ◄))

Que je fasse – *That I do*
Que tu fasses – *That you do*
Qu'il-elle fasse – *That he-she does*
Qu'on fasse – *That we do*
Que nous fassions – *That we do*
Que vous fassiez – *That you do*
Qu'ils-elles fassent – *That they do*

Futur proche

AUDIO 29.7

Je vais faire – *I am going to do*
Tu vas faire – *You are going to do*
Il-Elle va faire – *He-She is going to do*
On va faire – *We are going to do*
Nous allons faire – *We are going to do*
Vous allez faire – *You are going to do*
Ils-Elles vont faire – *They are going to do*

Passé récent

AUDIO 29.8

Je viens de faire – *I just did*
Tu viens de faire – *You just did*
Il-Elle vient de faire – *He-She just did*
On vient de faire – *We just did*
Nous venons de faire – *We just did*
Vous venez de faire – *You just did*
Ils-Elles viennent de faire – *They just did*

Impératif

AUDIO 29.9

Fais ! – *Do!*
Faisons ! – *Let's do!*
Faites ! – *Do!*

AUDIO 29.10

 Conjuguez le verbe **faire** au temps donné. Essayez de regarder le tableau de conjugaison avant et de compléter l'exercice de mémoire.
Conjugate the verb faire in the given tense. Try to look at the conjugation chart before and complete the exercise by memory.

1. **Présent de l'indicatif** : Je _____ du sport tous les jours.
   I exercise every day.

2. **Imparfait** : Quand on était enfants, on _____ toujours du vélo dans la rue.
   When we were kids, we always rode our bikes in the street.

3. **Futur simple** : Elle _____ de son mieux.
   She will do her best.

4. **Subjonctif présent** : C'est important que nous _____ attention à notre alimentation.
   It is important that we pay attention to our diet.

5. **Passé composé** : Hier, j'_____ du jogging dans le parc.
   Yesterday I went jogging in the park.

6.   attention de ne pas te brûler !

   Be careful not to burn yourself!

7. **Conditionnel présent** : Si j'avais plus de temps, je   du bénévolat.

   If I had more time, I would volunteer.

8. **Subjonctif présent** : Il faut que tu   des efforts pour réussir.

   You have to make an effort to succeed.

9. **Passé récent** : Je   toute la vaisselle.

   I just did all the dishes.

10. **Imparfait** : J'ai préparé le dîner pendant que tu   la sieste.

    I made dinner while you took a nap.

11. **Futur proche** : Elle   plus d'études mais elle ne sait pas encore quoi.

    She is going to do more studies but she doesn't know what yet.

12. **Subjonctif présent** : Il faut que tu   ton lit tous les matins.

    You have to make your bed every morning.

13. **Passé composé** : Pourquoi est-ce que tu   ça ?

    Why did you do that?

14. **Conditionnel présent** : Il   n'importe quoi pour recevoir une augmentation.

    He would do anything to get a raise.

15. **Futur simple** : Un jour, je   le tour du monde.

    One day, I will travel around the world.

RÉPONDRE AUX QUESTIONS AVEC OUI OU NON

30

ANSWER THE QUESTIONS WITH OUI OR NON

Answering question is a great exercise to practice your sentence building in French, especially with **oui** and **non**. The answer with **oui** is simple since you use the same sentence structure as the question, besides the subject pronoun and conjugation. Negative answers require to place the negation in the right spot. Do you remember the lesson about negation? If not, let's do a quick review!

AUDIO 30.1 ◀))

Simple negation *(not)* is made of two words in French: **ne** and **pas.**
Ne will be shortened to **n'** when the verb starts with a vowel or a silent h.

ne/n' + verb + pas

> **Je dors.** *I am sleeping.*
> **Je ne dors pas.** *I am not sleeping.*

When the verb is conjugated in **passé composé** or other **compound tenses**, the negation is placed around the auxiliary and is followed by the past participle.

ne/n' + auxiliary + pas + past participle

> **J'ai dormi.** *I slept.*
> **Je n'ai pas dormi.** *I didn't sleep.*

When **pas** is followed by an indefinite article « **un – une – des** » or a partitive article « **du – de la – de l' – des** », any of these articles become **de. De** becomes **d'** before a word starting with a vowel or a silent h.

ne + verb + pas + de/d'

> **Il regarde un film.** *He is watching a movie.*
> **Il ne regarde pas de film.** *He is not watching a movie.*

Répondez aux questions avec **oui** et **non**.
Answer the questions with oui and non.

1. **Est-ce que tu as faim ?**
   Are you hungry?

   Oui,

   Non,

2. **Est-ce que tu bois du café le matin ?**
   Do you drink coffee in the morning?

   Oui,

   Non,

3. **Est-ce que tu es né(e) en janvier ?**
   Were you born in January?

   Oui,

   Non,

4. **Est-ce que tu as un stylo ?**
   Do you have a pen?

   Oui,

   Non,

5. **Est-ce que tu as trouvé mon téléphone ?**
   Did you find my phone?

   Oui,

   Non,

6. **Est-ce que tu veux aller prendre un café ?**
   Do you want to go for coffee?

   Oui,

   Non,

7. **Est-ce que le train est à l'heure ?**
   Is the train on time?

   Oui,

   Non,

8. **Est-ce que le magasin est ouvert ?**
   Is the store open?

   Oui,

   Non,

9. **Est-ce que tu fais du sport ?**
   Do you exercise?

   Oui,

   Non,

10. **Est-ce que tu aimes la crème glacée ?**
    Do you like ice cream?

    Oui,

    Non,

11. **Est-ce que tu seras là ce soir ?**
    Will you be there this evening?

    Oui,

    Non,

12. **Est-ce que tu parles français ?**
    Do you speak French?

    Oui,

    Non,

13. **Est-ce que tu es heureux/heureuse ?**
    Are you happy?

    Oui,

    Non,

14. **Est-ce que tu sais nager ?**
Can you swim?

Oui,

Non,

15. **Est-ce que tu as fini de manger ?**
Have you finished eating?

Oui,

Non,

QUEL – QUELLE – QUELS – QUELLES
WHICH – WHAT

31

Quel and variations, are interrogative adjectives that translate to *which* and *what*.

French interrogative adjectives agree in gender and number with the noun they describe.

AUDIO 31.1 ◄))

Quel – Use **quel** before a masculine singular noun.

> **Quel examen** – *What exam*

Quelle – Use **quelle** before a feminine singular noun.

> **Quelle idée** – *What idea*

Quels – Use **quels** before a masculine plural.

> **Quels pays** – *What countries*

Quelles – Use **quelles** before a feminine plural noun.

> **Quelles maisons** – *What houses*

Quel and variations can be followed by a verb as well but it will always agree with the noun in the sentence.

———————————

AUDIO 31.2 ◄))

 Ajoutez **quel**, **quelle**, **quels** ou **quelles** à chaque phrase.
Add quel, quelle, quels, or quelles to each sentence.

1. _____ est ta matière préférée à l'école ?

   What is your favorite subject at school?

2. _____ est ton plat préféré ?

   What's your favorite dish?

3. _____ sont les pays que tu aimerais visiter ?

   Which countries would you like to visit?

4. _____ musiques est-ce que tu as choisies ?

What music did you choose?

5. _____ est la jupe que tu préfères ?

Which skirt do you prefer?

6. _____ habitudes est-ce que tu essayes de prendre ?

What habits are you trying to form?

7. _____ sont les livres que tu recommandes ?

What books do you recommend?

8. _____ est ton film préféré ?

What is your favorite movie?

9. _____ langues est-ce que tu parles ?

What languages do you speak?

10. _____ est ton opinion ?

What is your opinion?

11. _____ jour est-ce que tu es libre ?

What day are you free?

12. _____ est ta saison préférée ?

What is your favourite season?

13. _____ sont tes objectifs ?

What are your goals?

14. _____ est ton nom ?

What is your name?

15. _____ sont les villes que tu as visitées ?

Which cities have you visited?

L'ACCORD DE L'ADJECTIF

AGREEMENT OF THE ADJECTIVE

32

An adjective is a word that modifies or describes a noun. In other words, it helps to give information about the noun.

In French, adjectives agree in gender and number with the noun they modify or with the subject of the sentence, which will change the spelling and the pronunciation.

Adjectives Ending in -e

AUDIO 32.1 ◀))

When an adjective ends in **-e**, the masculine and feminine are the same. For the plural, add only an **-s**.

	Masc. sing.	Fem. sing.	Masc. pl.	Fem. pl.
Nice	**Agréable**	**Agréable**	**Agréables**	**Agréables**
Strange	**Bizarre**	**Bizarre**	**Bizarres**	**Bizarres**
Calm	**Calme**	**Calme**	**Calmes**	**Calmes**
Famous	**Célèbre**	**Célèbre**	**Célèbres**	**Célèbres**
Difficult	**Difficile**	**Difficile**	**Difficiles**	**Difficiles**
Funny	**Drôle**	**Drôle**	**Drôles**	**Drôles**
Easy	**Facile**	**Facile**	**Faciles**	**Faciles**
Weak	**Faible**	**Faible**	**Faibles**	**Faibles**
Young	**Jeune**	**Jeune**	**Jeunes**	**Jeunes**
Clean	**Propre**	**Propre**	**Propres**	**Propres**
Fast	**Rapide**	**Rapide**	**Rapides**	**Rapides**
Dirty	**Sale**	**Sale**	**Sales**	**Sales**
Shy	**Timide**	**Timide**	**Timides**	**Timides**
Sad	**Triste**	**Triste**	**Tristes**	**Tristes**
Empty	**Vide**	**Vide**	**Vides**	**Vides**

Adjectives Ending in -é -i -u

AUDIO 32.2 ◀))

When an adjective ends in **-é -i** or **-u**, the feminine will take an **-e**. For the plural, add only an **-s**.

Angry	**Fâché**	**Fâchée**	**Fâchés**	**Fâchées**
Tired	**Fatigué**	**Fatiguée**	**Fatigués**	**Fatiguées**
Pretty	**Joli**	**Jolie**	**Jolis**	**Jolies**
Polite	**Poli**	**Polie**	**Polis**	**Polies**
Delighted	**Ravi**	**Ravie**	**Ravis**	**Ravies**

Adjectives Ending in -t -d -n -s

When an adjective ends in **-t -d -n -s**, the feminine will take an **-e**. For the plural, add only an **-s**.

AUDIO 32.3 ◀))

Hot	Chaud	Chaude	Chauds	Chaudes
Happy	Content	Contente	Contents	Contentes
Strong	Fort	Forte	Forts	Fortes
Cold	Froid	Froide	Froids	Froides
Tall/Big	Grand	Grande	Grands	Grandes
Tall	Haut	Haute	Hauts	Hautes
Interesting	Intéressant	Intéressante	Intéressants	Intéressantes
Ugly	Laid	Laide	Laids	Laides
Slow	Lent	Lente	Lents	Lentes
Bad	Mauvais	Mauvaise	Mauvais	Mauvaises
Mean	Méchant	Méchante	Méchants	Méchantes
Best	Meilleur	Meilleure	Meilleurs	Meilleures
Small	Petit	Petite	Petits	Petites
Ready	Prêt	Prête	Prêts	Prêtes

*__mauvais__ doesn't change in masculine plural because French doesn't allow a double ss for plural.

Adjectives Ending in -eux

AUDIO 32.4 ◀))

When an adjective ends in **-eux**, the masculine singular and plural are the same, but the feminine forms turn into **-euse(s)**.

Brave	Courageux	Courageuse	Courageux	Courageuses
Happy	Heureux	Heureuse	Heureux	Heureuses
Serious	Sérieux	Sérieuse	Sérieux	Sérieuses

Adjectives Ending in -er

AUDIO 32.5 ◀))

When an adjective ends in **-er**, the feminine forms change to **-ère**.

Expensive	Cher	Chère	Chers	Chères
Last	Dernier	Dernière	Derniers	Dernières
First	Premier	Première	Premiers	Premières

Double Final Consonant

AUDIO 32.6 ◄))

Some adjectives will double the last consonant before adding an **-e** or an **-s** for the plural.

Kind	**Gentil**	**Gentille**	**Gentils**	**Gentilles**
Good	**Bon**	**Bonne**	**Bons**	**Bonnes**
Cute	**Mignon**	**Mignonne**	**Mignons**	**Mignonnes**

Adjectives with a Fifth Choice

Three adjectives have a specific ending if the following masculine noun starts with a vowel or a silent h. We will look more into them in chapter 34.

AUDIO 32.7 ◄))

	Masc. sing.	**Fem. Sing.**	**Masc. Sing.** **Vowel or silent h**	**Masc. Pl.**	**Fem. Pl.**
Beautiful	**Beau**	**Belle**	**Bel**	**Beaux**	**Belles**
New	**Nouveau**	**Nouvelle**	**Nouvel**	**Nouveaux**	**Nouvelles**
Old	**Vieux**	**Vieille**	**Vieil**	**Vieux**	**Vieilles**

Irregular adjectives

AUDIO 32.8 ◄))

Long	**Long**	**Longue**	**Longs**	**Longues**
Soft	**Doux**	**Douce**	**Doux**	**Douces**
White	**Blanc**	**Blanche**	**Blancs**	**Blanches**
Complete	**Complet**	**Complète**	**Complets**	**Complètes**
Wrong	**Faux**	**Fausse**	**Faux**	**Fausses**
Dry	**Sec**	**Sèche**	**Secs**	**Sèches**

AUDIO 32.9 ◄))

 Ajoutez **l'adjectif** en regardant à la traduction. N'oubliez pas de l'accorder avec le nom ou le sujet. Tous les adjectifs de cet exercice sont dans les listes ci-dessus.
Add the adjective by looking at the translation. Don't forget to match it with the name. All the adjectives in this exercise are in the lists above.

1. Ce problème est plus _____ que je ne le pensais.
    This problem is more difficult than I thought.

2. Il fait _____ aujourd'hui. On devrait aller à la plage.

It's hot today. We should go to the beach.

3. J'aime quand la maison est _____ .

I like it when the house is clean.

4. Le village où on est restés était _____ .

The village where we stayed was quiet.

5. Il est arrivé _____ au marathon.

He came first in the marathon.

6. Cette blague n'est pas _____ du tout.

This joke isn't funny at all.

7. J'étais _____ de te voir après autant de temps. (masculine)

I was delighted to see you after so long.

8. Il est toujours _____ après sa journée de travail.

He's always tired after his workday.

9. Ce pull est vraiment _____ .

This sweater is really soft.

10. Elle est _____ maintenant qu'elle a un _____ contrat.

She's happy now that she has a new contract.

11. Mon cousin est _____ depuis qu'il est _____ .

My cousin has been shy since he was little.

12. Paris est une _____ ville où il est _____ de se perdre.

Paris is a big city where it's easy to get lost.

13. Nous étions _____ d'apprendre la nouvelle.

We were sad to hear the news.

14. C'est la _____ glace de la ville.

It's the best ice cream in the city.

15. En hiver, il fait souvent _____ dans cette région.

In winter, it's often cold in this area.

OÙ PLACER LES ADJECTIFS

WHERE TO PLACE THE ADJECTIVES

33

In French, most adjectives are placed after the noun, which can be confusing for English speakers since the adjective is placed before the noun in English.

AUDIO 33.1 ◄))

Une fleur <u>blanche</u> – *A <u>white</u> flower*

However, just like most French rules, there are exceptions. Some adjectives are placed before the noun, and while there aren't that many that are placed before the noun, they are also the most common ones. Because of that, you will come across them a lot.

The adjectives placed before the noun usually express **Beauty**, **Age**, **Number**, **Goodness**, and **Size**. Remember it with the acronym **BANGS**.

Beauty

AUDIO 33.2 ◄))

	Masc. Sing.	Fem. Sing.	Masc. Pl.	Fem. Pl.
Beautiful	Beau	Belle	Beaux	Belles
Pretty	Joli	Jolie	Jolis	Jolies

Une <u>belle</u> voiture – *A beautiful car*
Un <u>joli</u> visage – *A pretty face*

Age

AUDIO 33.3 ◄))

	Masc. Sing.	Fem. Sing.	Masc. Pl.	Fem. Pl.
Young	Jeune	Jeune	Jeunes	Jeunes
Old	Vieux	Vieille	Vieux	Vieilles
New	Nouveau	Nouvelle	Nouveaux	Nouvelles

Une <u>vielle</u> personne – *On old person*
Un <u>nouveau</u> sac – *A new bag*

Number

AUDIO 33.4 ◄》

	Masc. Sing.	Fem. Sing.	Masc. Pl.	Fem. Pl.
First	Premier	Première	Premiers	Premières
Second	Deuxième	Deuxième	Deuxièmes	Deuxièmes
Last	Dernier	Dernière	Derniers	Dernières

Le **dernier** passager – *The last passenger*
Mon **premier** chien – *My first dog*

Goodness

AUDIO 33.5 ◄》

	Masc. Sing.	Fem. Sing.	Masc. Pl.	Fem. Pl.
Good	Bon	Bonne	Bons	Bonnes
Bad	Mauvais	Mauvaise	Mauvais	Mauvaises
Best/Better	Meilleur	Meilleure	Meilleurs	Meilleures
Kind/Nice	Gentil	Gentille	Gentils	Gentilles

Une **bon** gâteau – *A good cake*
Un **mauvais** investissement – *A bad investment*
Une **meilleure** idée – *A better idea*
Un **gentil** monsieur – *A nice man*

Size

AUDIO 33.6 ◄》

	Masc. Sing.	Fem. Sing.	Masc. Pl.	Fem. Pl.
Small	Petit	Petite	Petits	Petites
Tall	Grand	Grande	Grands	Grandes
Big	Gros	Grosse	Gros	Grosses
Long	Long	Longue	Longs	Longues

Un **petit** oiseau – *A small bird*
Un **grand** immeuble – *A tall building*
Une **grosse** bêtise – *A big mistake*
Un **long** chemin – *A long way*

Ajoutez **l'adjectif** donné **avant** ou **après** le nom. Accordez l'adjectif si besoin.
Add the adjective before or after the noun. Change the adjective depending on the gender and number.

1. **Beau** – Quel   manteau   !
   What a beautiful coat!

2. **Chaud** – J'ai besoin d'une   douche   .
   I need a warm shower.

3. **Vieux** – Mon voisin est un   homme   .
   My neighbor is an old man.

4. **Nouveau** – Est-ce que tu as reçu ta   carte d'identité   ?
   Have you received your new ID card?

5. **Libre** – Il y a des   places   au premier rang.
   There are free seats in the front row.

6. **Meilleur** – C'est la   tarte   que j'aie mangée.
   It's the best pie I've ever eaten.

7. **Troisième** – Il a réussi la   fois   qu'il a essayé.
   He succeeded the third time he tried.

8. **Effrayant** – Il a lu une   histoire   aux enfants.
   He read a scary story to the children.

9. **Dernier** – C'était sa   journée   au travail.
   It was his last day at work.

10. **Bon** – Elle a toujours une   excuse   .
    She always has a good excuse.

11. **Vrai** – Ce film est basé sur une   histoire   .
    This movie is based on a true story.

12. **Vert** – Le   pull   te va mieux que le noir.
    The green sweater looks better on you than the black one.

13. **Heureux** – C'est un   moment   pour toute la famille.
It's a happy moment for the whole family.

14. **Petit** – Elle est toujours avec son   chien   .
She's always with her small dog.

15. **Rouge** – Son rêve était d'acheter une   voiture   .
Her dream was to buy a red car.

BEAU – NOUVEAU – VIEUX

BEAUTIFUL – NEW – OLD

34

Beau, **nouveau** and **vieux** are specific adjectives in French. French adjectives have
4 different forms: masculine singular – feminine singular – masculine plural –
feminine plural. **Beau, nouveau,** and **vieux** are different. They have 5 different forms.
The fifth form *(here placed third)* **is when a masculine noun starts with a vowel or a silent h.**

Let's learn them or review them!

AUDIO 34.1 ◀))

	Masculine Singular	Feminine Singular	Masc. Sing. Vowel or Silent H	Masculine Plural	Feminine Plural
Beautiful	Beau	Belle	Bel	Beaux	Belles
New	Nouveau	Nouvelle	Nouvel	Nouveaux	Nouvelles
Old	Vieux	Vieille	Vieil	Vieux	Vieilles

Un <u>nouveau</u> chargeur – *A new charger*
Un <u>nouvel</u> outil – *A new tool*

Un <u>vieux</u> proverbe – *An old proverb*
Un <u>vieil</u> appartement – *An old apartment*

Un <u>beau</u> meuble – *A beautiful piece of furniture*
Un <u>bel</u> homme – *A beautiful man*

AUDIO 34.2 ◀))

 En regardant la traduction, ajoutez **le bon adjectif** à chaque phrase. Accordez
l'adjectif si besoin.
*Looking at the translation, add the correct adjective to each sentence. Change the
adjective depending on the gender and number.*

1. La _____ maison en pierre va être rénovée.

    The old stone house is going to be renovated.

2. Mes _____ chaussures sont arrivées ce matin.

    My new shoes arrived this morning.

3. Ce bâtiment est un _____ exemple d'architecture.

    This building is a beautiful example of architecture.

4. C'est un   bouquet de fleurs ?

   Is this a new bouquet of flowers?

5. Ses meubles ont l'air   mais ils sont   .

   His furniture looks old but it's new.

6. C'est un   endroit pour se promener.

   It's a beautiful place to walk around.

7. Elle porte un   collier.

   She wears an old necklace.

8. La maison qu'on a visitée est   .

   The house we visited is beautiful.

9. Est-ce que tu as reçu le   horaire ?

   Have you received the new schedule?

10. Le   homme qui habitait ici est décédé.

    The old man who lived here died.

11. Les   arrivants reçoivent un sac cadeau.

    New arrivals receive a gift bag.

12. Il a un   sourire.

    He has a beautiful smile.

13. Ta   jupe est vraiment   .

    Your new skirt is really beautiful.

14. Pascal est un   ami.

    Pascal is an old friend.

15. C'est une   histoire d'amour.

    It's a beautiful love story.

TROUVEZ LES ERREURS

FIND THE ERRORS

35

Time for a recap! Here are 15 questions related to everything we have seen from chapter 24 to the last chapter. Each answer is explained in the solutions.

AUDIO 35.1 🔊

 Trouvez **les erreurs** dans les phrases ci-dessous.
Find the errors in the sentences below.

1. Qu'est-ce que tu fait ce soir ?
   What are you doing tonight?

2. La nouveau édition vient juste de sortir.
   The new edition has just been released.

3. Il veut qu'on parle de la projet avant la réunion.
   He wants us to talk about the project before the meeting.

4. Est-ce que tu sais jouer à piano ?
   Do you know how to play the piano?

5. Est-ce que tu as eu le temps de préparer le dîner ? Non, j'ai eu le temps de préparer le dîner.
   Did you have time to prepare dinner? No, I didn't have time to prepare dinner.

6. Il a réussi de changer ses pneus tout seul.
   He managed to change his tires on his own.

7. J'ai lu ce vieux article hier soir.
   I read this old article last night.

8. Notre voyage à l'Australie était incroyable.
   Our trip to Australia was incredible.

9. J'ai faire du café. Est-ce que tu en veux ?
   I made coffee. Do you want some?

10. Quel glace est-ce que tu veux ?
    What ice cream do you want?

11. Elle est souvent pensif.
    She is often pensive.

12. C'est un belle tableau que tu as peint.
    It's a beautiful picture you painted.

13. J'ai envie un chocolat chaud pour me réchauffer.
    I want some hot chocolate to warm me up.

14. Pourquoi est-ce que tu refuses à leur parler ?
    Why do you refuse to talk to them?

15. Est-ce que vous êtes déjà allés au États-Unis ?
    Have you ever been to the United States?

LE BON ADJECTIF AVEC ÊTRE
THE RIGHT ADJECTIVE WITH ÊTRE

36

Finding an adjective after the verb **être** (*To be*) is common in French, even in English. An adjective placed after **être** agrees in gender and number with the subject.

AUDIO 36.1 🔊

Ce pull est <u>blanc</u>. *This sweater is white.*
Cette robe est <u>blanche</u>. *This dress is white.*

In the examples above, we can see that the adjective **blanc** agrees with the subject and changes to blanche since **cette robe** is feminine singular.

Go back to chapter 32 to review how adjectives change when masculine, feminine, singular and plural.

AUDIO 36.2 🔊

 Choisissez **le bon adjectif** en fonction du genre et du nombre du sujet.
Choose the right adjective based on the gender and number of the subject.

1. **français – française** – Je pense qu'elle est _____ mais je ne suis pas sûre.
    I think she's French but I'm not sure.

2. **certains – certain** – Tu es _____ de ce que tu dis ?
    Are you sure of what you are saying?

3. **seul – seule** – Elle est la _____ à m'avoir répondu.
    She was the only one who answered me.

4. **nombreux – nombreuses** – Les joueurs sont _____ à participer.
    Many players participate.

5. **heureux – heureuse** – Elle est _____ pour la première fois depuis longtemps.
    She is happy for the first time in a long time.

---

6. **social – sociale** – Il n'a jamais été très   .
   He was never very social.

7. **petits – petites** – Ces pneus sont plus   que je ne le pensais.
   These tires are smaller than I thought.

8. **difficile – difficiles** – Ce questionnaire est vraiment   .
   This quiz is really difficult.

9. **ouverts – ouvertes** – Les portes seront   à 9 heures du matin.
   Doors will open at 9 a.m.

10. **déçu – déçue** – On espère qu'il n'est pas   de ses résultats.
    We hope he is not disappointed with his results.

11. **craintif – craintive** – Mon chat est   depuis qu'il est petit.
    My cat has been fearful since he was little.

12. **fou – folle** – C'est une idée complètement   .
    This is a completely crazy idea.

13. **désolé – désolée** – Il est   de t'avoir fait de la peine.
    He's sorry for hurting you.

14. **créatifs – créatif** – Mes enfants sont toujours   .
    My children are always creative.

15. **précis – précises** – Est-ce que ces mesures sont   ?
    Are these measurements accurate?

L'IMPARFAIT

THE IMPERFECT

37

In this review and exercise, we are going to change verbs into the **imparfait**. Let's review when to use the **imparfait** and the conjugation of verbs.

When to Use the Imparfait

The **imparfait** is used to talk about the past, mostly actions and situations without a specific timeframe that happened an unspecified number of times or were in progress when something else happened.

AUDIO 37.1 ◀))

J'adorais jouer au football quand j'étais petit.
I loved playing soccer when I was little.

Building the Imparfait

To form the **imparfait**, we need to find the stem of the verb. To do this, we will look at the verb conjugated in the present tense with **nous**, remove the **-ons** and add the endings for the imparfait: **-ais**, **-ais**, **-ait**, **-ions**, **-iez** and **-aient**. **Être** is the only verb not following the stem rule.

Conjugation of Verbs in the Imparfait

Let's conjugate a verb of the 1st group ending in **-er** as an example.

AUDIO 37.2 ◀))

Porter – *To wear*   Nous portons   Stem: **port-**

Pr.	Stem + Endings	Conjugated verb	Translation
Je	port – **ais**	**Je portais**	*I wore – I was wearing*
Tu	port – **ais**	**Tu portais**	*You wore – You were wearing*
Il-Elle-On	port – **ait**	**Il-Elle-On portait**	*He-She wore – He-She was wearing*
Nous	port – **ions**	**Nous portions**	*We wore – We were wearing*
Vous	port – **iez**	**Vous portiez**	*You wore – You were wearing*
Ils-Elles	port – **aient**	**Ils-Elles portaient**	*They wore – They were wearing*

Verb	Présent	Imparfait – Je	Imparfait – Nous
Apprendre *To learn*	Nous **apprenons**	J'apprenais	**Nous apprenions**
Avoir *To have*	Nous **avons**	J'avais	**Nous avions**
Boire *To drink*	Nous **buvons**	Je buvais	**Nous buvions**
Écrire *To write*	Nous **écrivons**	J'écrivais	**Nous écrivions**
Faire *To do*	Nous **faisons**	Je faisais	**Nous faisions**
Finir *To finish*	Nous **finissons**	Je finissais	**Nous finissions**
Goûter *To taste*	Nous **goûtons**	Je goûtais	**Nous goûtions**
Habiter *To live*	Nous **habitons**	J'habitais	**Nous habitions**
Nettoyer *To clean*	Nous **nettoyons**	Je nettoyais	**Nous nettoyions**
Oublier *To forget*	Nous **oublions**	J'oubliais	**Nous oubliions**
Passer *To spend*	Nous **passons**	Je passais	**Nous passions**
Porter *To wear*	Nous **portons**	Je portais	**Nous portions**
Réserver *To book*	Nous **réservons**	Je réservais	**Nous réservions**
Vendre *To sell*	Nous **vendons**	Je vendais	**Nous vendions**
Vouloir *To want*	Nous **voulons**	Je voulais	**Nous voulions**

The verb **être** is the only one that doesn't use the present tense stem:

Être – *To be*

J'**étais**	Nous **étions**
Tu **étais**	Vous **étiez**
Il-Elle-On **était**	Ils-Elles **étaient**

 Réécrivez les phrases en conjuguant le verbe à **l'imparfait**. Pour vous aider, vous pouvez écrire le verbe à l'infinitif et le conjuguer au présent.
Rewrite the sentences by conjugating the verb in the imperfect tense. To help you, you can write the verb in the infinitive and conjugate it in the present tense.

1. J'ai 25 ans.
   I am 25 years old.

   Infinitif :   Présent de l'indicatif : Nous

2. On habite à la campagne.
We live in the countryside.

Infinitif :   Présent de l'indicatif : Nous

3. Pourquoi est-ce que tu ne veux pas aller en vacances ?
Why don't you want to go on vacation?

Infinitif :   Présent de l'indicatif : Nous

4. Cet auteur écrit un peu tous les jours.
This author writes a little every day.

Infinitif :   Présent de l'indicatif : Nous

5. C'est une belle journée pour une promenade.
It's a beautiful day for a walk.

Infinitif :   Présent de l'indicatif : Nous

6. Elle porte des lunettes pour lire.
She wears glasses to read.

Infinitif :   Présent de l'indicatif : Nous

7. Nous passons une agréable journée à la plage.
We are spending a pleasant day at the beach.

Infinitif :   Présent de l'indicatif : Nous

8. Ce magasin vend des habits et des chaussures.
This store sells clothes and shoes.

Infinitif :   Présent de l'indicatif : Nous

9. Mes parents réservent toujours leurs vacances en dernière minute.
   My parents always book their vacations last minute.

   Infinitif :   Présent de l'indicatif : Nous

10. Je bois du café tous les matins.
    I drink coffee every morning.

    Infinitif :   Présent de l'indicatif : Nous

11. Il fait beau.
    The weather is good.

    Infinitif :   Présent de l'indicatif : Nous

12. Les élèves apprennent un peu de français quotidiennement.
    Students learn a little French daily.

    Infinitif :   Présent de l'indicatif : Nous

13. On nettoie la maison une fois par semaine.
    We clean the house once a week.

    Infinitif :   Présent de l'indicatif : Nous

14. Elle goûte toujours tout quand elle cuisine.
    She always tastes everything when she cooks.

    Infinitif :   Présent de l'indicatif : Nous

    Infinitif :   Présent de l'indicatif : Nous

15. Il oublie toujours quelque chose à la maison.
    He always forgets something at home.

    Infinitif :   Présent de l'indicatif : Nous

J'AI MAL ...

MY ... HURT

38

Describing aches and pain is important in any language you speak. In French, the sentence structure is different than in English. While in English, you either start with the part of the body follow by the verb *"hurt"* or *"I have a"*, in French, we start by **"J'ai mal + à"**, which translate to *"I have pain in"*.

Avoir mal is followed by the preposition **à** in French. As we saw before, the preposition **à** changes depending on if the following noun is masculine, feminine, or plural.

AUDIO 38.1 ◀))

avoir mal à + le = **au** + singular masculine noun

    avoir mal au genou – *to have knee pain*

avoir mal à + les = **aux** + plural masculine or feminine noun

    avoir mal aux dents – *to have a toothache*

avoir mal à + la = **à la** + singular feminine noun

    avoir mal à la tête – *to have a headache*

avoir mal à + l' = **à l'** + singular masculine or feminine noun starting with a vowel or a silent h

    avoir mal à l'oreille – *to have an earache*

AUDIO 38.2 ◀))

Here is a list of the common aches you can have:

Avoir mal à l'estomac	*To have a stomachache*
Avoir mal à la gorge	*To have a sore throat*
Avoir mal à la poitrine	*To have chest pain*
Avoir mal à la tête	*To have a headache*
Avoir mal au cœur	*To have a heartache*
Avoir mal au cou	*To have neck pain*
Avoir mal au dos	*To have back pain*
Avoir mal au ventre	*To have a stomachache*
Avoir mal aux bras / au bras	*To have arms pain/arm pain*
Avoir mal aux chevilles / à la cheville	*To have ankles/ankle pain*
Avoir mal aux coudes / au coude	*To have pain in your elbows/elbow*
Avoir mal aux dents	*To have a toothache*

Avoir mal aux doigts / au doigt	*To have pain in your fingers/finger*
Avoir mal aux épaules / à l'épaule	*To have shoulders/shoulder pain*
Avoir mal aux gencives	*To have sore gums*
Avoir mal aux hanches / à la hanche	*To have pain in the hips/in the hip*
Avoir mal aux jambes / à la jambe	*To have legs/leg pain*
Avoir mal aux mains / à la main	*To have pain in your hands*
Avoir mal aux muscles	*To have muscle pain*
Avoir mal aux oreilles / à l'oreille	*To have earache/ear pain*
Avoir mal aux orteils / à l'orteil	*To have pain in your toes/toe*
Avoir mal aux pieds / au pied	*To have pain in your feet/foot*
Avoir mal aux poignets / au poignet	*To have pain in the wrists/wrist*
Avoir mal aux yeux / à l'œil	*To have pain in the eyes/eye*

AUDIO 38.3 ◀))

 Ajoutez **la bonne partie du corps** en regardant à la traduction. Faites attention à la traduction pour voir si c'est singulier ou pluriel.
Add the right part of the body by looking at the translation. Pay attention to the translation to see if it's singular or plural.

1. J'ai mal _____ .

   I have a sore throat.

2. J'ai mal _____ .

   I have a stomachache.

3. J'ai mal _____ .

   I have a headache.

4. J'ai mal _____ .

   I have an earache.

5. J'ai mal _____ .

   I have a toothache.

6. J'ai mal _____ .

   My feet hurt.

7. J'ai mal _____ .

   My finger hurts.

8. J'ai mal   .

   My leg hurts.

9. J'ai mal   .

   My wrist hurts.

10. J'ai mal   .

   My neck hurts.

LE FUTUR SIMPLE

THE FUTURE TENSE

39

The future tense, called **futur simple** in French, is the equivalent of *will* in English.

AUDIO 39.1 🔊

On <u>sera</u> au restaurant à 19 heures.
We <u>will be</u> at the restaurant at 7 p.m.

Using and Building the Futur Simple

In English, you add *will* in front of the verb, but in French, we add endings to the infinitive verb for verbs ending in **-er** and **-ir**. For verbs ending in **-re**, we remove the final **-e** before adding the endings. The endings for the futur simple are: **-ai**, **-as**, **-a**, **-ons**, **-ez** and **-ont**.

Let's conjugate a verb of the 1st group ending in **-er** as an example.

AUDIO 39.2 🔊

Chanter – *To sing*

Pr.	Stem + Endings	Conjugated verb	Translation
Je	chanter – **ai**	**Je chanterai**	*I will sing*
Tu	chanter – **as**	**Tu chanteras**	*You will sing*
Il-Elle-On	chanter – **a**	**Il-Elle-On chantera**	*He-She will sing*
Nous	chanter – **ons**	**Nous chanterons**	*We will sing*
Vous	chanter – **ez**	**Vous chanterez**	*You will sing*
Ils-Elles	chanter – **ont**	**Ils-Elles chanteront**	*They will sing*

AUDIO 39.3 🔊

Ouvrir – *To open*	**Ouvrir + endings**
J'ouvrirai	*I will open*
Tu ouvriras	*You will open*
Il-Elle-On ouvrira	*He-She-We will open*
Nous ouvrirons	*We will open*
Vous ouvrirez	*You will open*
Ils-Elles ouvriront	*They will open*

Rendre – *To give back* | **Rendr + endings** (remember to remove the final -e)

Je rendrai	*I will give back*
Tu rendras	*You will give back*
Il-Elle-On rendra	*He-She-We will give back*
Nous rendrons	*We will give back*
Vous rendrez	*You will give back*
Ils-Elles rendront	*They will give back*

Other irregular verbs and compounds are also irregular when conjugated in the **futur simple**:

Aller	*To go*	**J'irai – Nous irons – Ils iront**
Avoir	*To have*	**J'aurai – Nous aurons – Ils auront**
Devoir	*To have to*	**Je devrai – Nous devrons – Ils devront**
Être	*To be*	**Je serai – Nous serons – Ils seront**
Faire	*To do/to make*	**Je ferai – Nous ferons – Ils feront**
Pouvoir	*To be able to*	**Je pourrai – Nous pourrons – Ils pourront**
Savoir	*To know*	**Je saurai – Nous saurons – Ils sauront**
Tenir	*To hold*	**Je tiendrai – Nous tiendrons – Ils tiendront**
Venir	*To come*	**Je viendrai – Nous viendrons – Ils viendront**
Voir	*To see*	**Je verrai – Nous verrons – Ils verront**
Vouloir	*To want*	**Je voudrai – Nous voudrons – Ils voudront**

 Conjuguer **le verbe donné** au **futur simple**.
Conjugate the given verb in the future tense.

1. **Regarder** – On ⬚⬚⬚⬚⬚⬚ ce film ce week-end.

   We will watch this movie this weekend.

2. **Faire** – Ma grand-mère ⬚⬚⬚⬚⬚⬚ mon gâteau préféré pour mon anniversaire.

   My grandmother will make my favorite cake for my birthday.

3. **Téléphoner** – Je ⬚⬚⬚⬚⬚⬚ à mon amie après le travail.

   I'll call my friend after work.

4. **Venir** – Mes petits-enfants _____ me rendre visite bientôt.

   My grandchildren will come to visit me soon.

5. **Chercher** – Je _____ un nouveau travail quand j'en aurai besoin.

   I will look for a new job when I need it.

6. **Rendre** – Elle te _____ ton livre quand elle l'aura fini.

   She will give you back your book when she is done with it.

7. **Arriver** – Le bus _____ aux alentours de 10 heures.

   The bus will arrive around 10 a.m.

8. **Finir** – Les enfants _____ leurs devoirs avant le dîner.

   The children will finish their homework before dinner.

9. **Lire** – Je _____ ton livre pendant les vacances.

   I will read your book during the holidays.

10. **Dormir** – Nous _____ dans une auberge de jeunesse pendant le voyage.

    We will sleep in a youth hostel during the trip.

11. **Manger** – Je _____ moins de sucre demain.

    I will eat less sugar tomorrow.

12. **Parler** – On _____ à notre banquier pour un nouveau crédit.

    We will speak to our banker about a new loan.

13. **Montrer** – Je te _____ comment faire.

    I'll show you how to do it.

14. **Voir** – Tu _____, c'est plus facile que tu ne le penses.

    You'll see, it's easier than you think.

15. **Aller** – J'_____ peut-être avec elle au cinéma.

    Maybe I'll go with her to the cinema.

LE FUTUR PROCHE

THE NEAR FUTURE

40

The near future is called **futur proche** in French, simply because it's going to happen in the near future.

AUDIO 40.1 ◀))

On **va partir** dans quelques minutes.
We are going to leave in a few minutes.

Using and Building the Futur Proche

To build the **futur proche**, all you need to do is to conjugate the verb **aller** in the present tense and add the infinitive verb of the action you want to describe.

Let's conjugate the verb **aller** in the present tense.

AUDIO 40.2 ◀))

Aller – *To go*

Je **vais**	Nous **allons**
Tu **vas**	Vous **allez**
Il-Elle On **va**	Ils-Elles **vont**

Examples

AUDIO 40.3 ◀))

Nous allons mettre notre maison en vente.
We are going to put our house up for sale.

Je vais me changer.
I'm going to change.

Changez le verbe de la phrase **du futur simple** au **futur proche**. Vous pouvez aussi ajouter l'infinitif du verbe entre parenthèses.
Change the verb in the sentence from the simple future to the near future. You can also add the infinitive of the verb in parentheses.

1. Ils auront la réponse de l'avocat demain matin.
   They will have the lawyer's response tomorrow morning.

   Ils   la réponse de l'avocat demain matin.

   (   )

2. Le chanteur arrivera à l'hôtel dans quelques heures.
   The singer will arrive at the hotel in a few hours.

   Le chanteur   à l'hôtel dans quelques heures.

   (   )

3. Demain, je visiterai Rome.
   Tomorrow I will visit Rome.

   Demain, je   Rome. (   )

4. Elle écrira un livre sur son voyage.
   She will write a book about her trip.

   Elle   un livre sur son voyage. (   )

5. On ira au cinéma après les cours.
   We'll go to the cinema after school.

   On   au cinéma après les cours. (   )

6. Tu verras si tu veux venir avec nous.
   You'll see if you want to come with us.

   Tu   si tu veux venir avec nous. (   )

7. Est-ce que tu rendras l'argent à tes parents ?
   Will you return the money to your parents?

   Est-ce que tu   l'argent à tes parents ?

   (   )

8. Je regarderai dans ma chambre si je trouve ton téléphone.
I'll check my room if I find your phone.

Je _____ dans ma chambre si je trouve ton téléphone.

(_____)

9. Les professeurs prépareront les collations pour la journée.
Teachers will prepare snacks for the day.

Les professeurs _____ les collations pour la journée.

(_____)

10. On sera quelques minutes en retard.
We'll be a few minutes late.

On _____ quelques minutes en retard. (_____)

11. Les clients de l'hôtel pourront utiliser la piscine demain.
Hotel guests will be able to use the swimming pool tomorrow.

Les clients de l'hôtel _____ utiliser la piscine demain.

(_____)

12. Il faudra relire les documents avant de les signer.
You will need to reread the documents before signing them.

Il _____ relire les documents avant de les signer.

(_____)

13. Tu prendras ton sac avec toi ?
Will you take your bag with you?

Tu _____ ton sac avec toi ? (_____)

14. Il devra accepter les règles de sa nouvelle école.
He will have to accept the rules of his new school.

Il _____ accepter les règles de sa nouvelle école.

(_____)

15. Le pianiste jouera son morceau le plus célèbre.
The pianist will play his most famous piece.

Le pianiste _____ son morceau le plus célèbre. (_____)

RÉCAPITULATIF DE CONJUGAISON
CONJUGATION RECAP

41

We have seen a lot of conjugation in this book so let's do an exercise to review!

AUDIO 41.1 🔊

Conjuguez **le verbe** au temps donné pour chaque phrase.
Conjugate the verb in the given tense for each sentence.

1. **Courir – Passé composé**

   Il _____ pour attraper le bus mais le bus ne l'a pas attendu.

   He ran to catch the bus but the bus didn't wait for him.

2. **Avoir – Futur simple**

   Tu _____ de la chance si tu gagnes le gros lot.

   You'll be lucky if you win the jackpot.

3. **Être – Présent**

   Vous _____ toujours les bienvenus.

   You are always welcome.

4. **Plaire – Passé composé**

   Est-ce que ce film t' _____ ?

   Did you like this movie?

5. **Faire – Présent**

   Nous _____ du vélo ensemble quand il fait beau.

   We cycle together when the weather is nice.

6. **Prendre – Passé composé**

   Tu _____ des cours de danse quand tu étais petite ?

   Did you take dance lessons when you were little?

7. **Annoncer – Futur simple**

   Ils _____ le gagnant après le tirage.

   They will announce the winner after the drawing.

8. **Devoir – Imparfait**

   On _____ se voir hier mais elle a annulé.

   We were supposed to meet yesterday but she canceled.

9. **Estimer – Passé composé**

   L'agent immobilier _____ la maison pour la vendre.

   The real estate agent valued the house to sell it.

10. **Falloir – Présent**

    Il _____ que tu prennes soin de toi.

    You need to take care of yourself.

11. **Pouvoir – Futur simple**

    Je _____ t'aider avec tes devoirs après le dîner.

    I can help you with your homework after dinner.

12. **Aller – Conditionnel présent**

    J' _____ au restaurant plus souvent si je pouvais.

    I would go to restaurants more often if I could.

13. **Prévoir – Passé composé**

    Tu _____ assez de temps pour étudier ?

    Have you planned enough time to study?

14. **Rendre – Futur proche**

    On _____ visite à mes grands-parents ce soir.

    We're going to visit my grandparents this evening.

15. **Venir – Passé composé**

    Harry _____ avec nous au concert.

    Harry came with us to the concert.

L'OBJET DIRECT ET LE PRONOM D'OBJET DIRECT

42

DIRECT OBJECT AND
DIRECT OBJECT PRONOUN

In French, a direct object (**Complément d'Objet Direct = COD**) is a group of words directly receiving the verb's action. It answers the questions "**Quoi ?** *(what?)*" or "**Qui ?** *(who?)*."

AUDIO 42.1 ◄))

Je mange une pomme. *I am eating an apple.*
Je mange quoi ? *What am I eating?*
= **Une pomme** – *An apple* is the direct object.

A direct object pronoun replaces the direct object to avoid repetition.

Here are the direct object pronouns in French:

AUDIO 42.2 ◄))

Singular	Plural
me – m' – *me*	**nous** – *us*
te – t' – *you*	**vous** – *you*
le – l' – *him/it*	**les** – *them*
la – l' – *her/it*	

If we look at the example above, **une pomme** is the direct object. The direct object pronoun is **la** since une pomme is feminine singular.

Je mange une pomme. *I am eating an apple.*
Direct object: **une pomme**   Direct object pronoun: **la**

AUDIO 42.3 ◄))

  Trouvez **l'objet direct** dans la phrase et transformez-le en **pronom**.
Find the direct object in the sentence and change it into a pronoun.

1. Est-ce que tu as vu ce film ?
    Have you seen this movie?

    Direct object: Direct object pronoun:

2. On prépare le dîner ensemble.
We're preparing dinner together.

Direct object: Direct object pronoun:

3. Le chat a attrapé la souris.
The cat caught the mouse.

Direct object: Direct object pronoun:

4. J'ai perdu mes clés.
I've lost my keys.

Direct object: Direct object pronoun:

5. Il a acheté ces fleurs pour sa femme.
He bought these flowers for his wife.

Direct object: Direct object pronoun:

6. Mon chien cherche son os dans le jardin.
My dog is searching for his bone in the garden.

Direct object: Direct object pronoun:

7. On voit mon frère dans la foule.
We see my brother in the crowd.

Direct object: Direct object pronoun:

8. J'ai appelé Julie mais elle n'a pas répondu.
I called Julie but she didn't answer.

Direct object: Direct object pronoun:

9. Nous avons attendu le train mais il a été annulé.
We waited for the train but it was canceled.

Direct object: Direct object pronoun:

10. Elle a adoré ses cadeaux.
She loved her gifts.

Direct object: Direct object pronoun:

11. On a écouté sa nouvelle chanson.
We listened to his new song.

Direct object: Direct object pronoun:

12. J'attends Sarah pour aller faire un jogging.
I'm waiting for Sarah to go jogging.

Direct object: Direct object pronoun:

13. Les élèves écoutent le professeur.
The students are listening to the teacher.

Direct object: Direct object pronoun:

14. Tu as compris la leçon ?
Did you understand the lesson?

Direct object: Direct object pronoun:

15. Elle a commandé sa nouvelle robe.
She ordered her new dress.

Direct object: Direct object pronoun:

LE PRONOM D'OBJET DIRECT – PLACE ET ACCORD

43

DIRECT OBJECT PRONOUN – PLACE AND AGREEMENT

Now that we have seen how to transform a direct object into a direct object pronoun, let's have a look at where to place it and how it can change the verb in some cases.

Place of the Direct Object Pronoun in a Simple Sentence

The direct object pronoun is placed before the verb in a simple sentence. In English, the pronoun stays after the verb. This is different in French.

Subject + DOP + verb

Let's see the same example used in the previous exercise.

AUDIO 43.1 ◄))

> **Je mange une pomme.** *I am eating an apple.*
> **une pomme** – *An apple* is the direct object.
> = **la** is the direct object pronoun

If we placed the direct object pronoun before the verb, here is what we have:

> **Je <u>la</u> mange.** *I am eating <u>it</u>.*

Place of the Direct Object Pronoun in Compound Tenses

When a verb is conjugated in a compound tense with **avoir**, the past participle agrees with the direct object pronoun in gender and number.

Subject + DOP + auxiliary + past participle + -.e.s.es

AUDIO 43.2 ◄))

If the pronoun is masculine singular, add nothing to the past participle.

J'ai mangé <u>un croissant</u> = Je l'ai mangé
I ate a croissant = I ate it

If the pronoun is feminine singular, add **-e** to the past participle.

>**J'ai mangé <u>une pomme</u> = Je l'ai mangé<u>e</u>**
>*I ate an apple = I ate it*

If the pronoun is masculine plural, add **-s** to the past participle.

>**J'ai mangé <u>deux croissants</u> = Je <u>les</u> ai mangé<u>s</u>**
>*I ate two croissants = I ate them*

If the pronoun is feminine plural, add **-es** to the past participle.

>**J'ai mangé <u>deux pommes</u> = Je <u>les</u> ai mangé<u>es</u>**
>*I ate two apples = I ate them*

AUDIO 43.3 ◀))

 Continuons l'exercice précédent. Changez **l'objet direct** en **pronom** et **accordez** le participe passé si besoin.
Let's continue the previous exercise. Change the direct object to a pronoun and add the agreement to the past participle if necessary.

1. Est-ce que tu as vu ce film ?
   Have you seen this movie?

   Have you seen it?

2. On prépare le dîner ensemble.
   We're preparing dinner together.

   We're preparing it together.

3. Le chat a attrapé la souris.
   The cat caught the mouse.

   The cat caught it.

4. J'ai perdu mes clés.
   I've lost my keys.

   I've lost them.

5. Il a acheté ces fleurs pour sa femme.
   He bought these flowers for his wife.

   He bought them for his wife.

6. Mon chien cherche son os dans le jardin.
   My dog is searching for his bone in the garden.

   My dog is searching for it in the garden.

7. On voit mon frère dans la foule.
   We see my brother in the crowd.

   We see him in the crowd.

8. J'ai appelé Julie mais elle n'a pas répondu.
   I called Julie but she didn't answer.

   I called her but she didn't answer.

9. Nous avons attendu le train mais il a été annulé.
   We waited for the train but it was canceled.

   We waited for it but it was canceled.

10. Elle a adoré ses cadeaux.
    She loved her gifts.

    She loved them.

11. On a écouté sa nouvelle chanson.
    We listened to his new song.

    We listened to it.

12. J'attends Sarah pour aller faire un jogging.
I'm waiting for Sarah to go jogging.

I'm waiting for her to go jogging.

13. Les élèves écoutent le professeur.
The students are listening to the teacher.

The students are listening to him.

14. Tu as compris la leçon ?
Did you understand the lesson?

Did you understand it?

15. Elle a commandé sa nouvelle robe.
She ordered her new dress.

She ordered it.

L'OBJET INDIRECT ET LE PRONOM D'OBJET DIRECT

44

INDIRECT OBJECT AND INDIRECT OBJECT PRONOUN

What is an Indirect Object?

An indirect object is a group of words preceded by the preposition **à**. We found the indirect object by asking the question **à qui ?** *(to whom?)*.

AUDIO 44.1 ◀))

Je parle à ma mère. *I am talking to my mother.*
Je parle à qui ? *Who am I talking to?*
= **à ma mère** – *to my mother* is the indirect object.

Indirect Object Pronouns

An indirect object pronoun replaces the indirect object and is placed before the verb, or before the auxiliary and the past participle. We use them the same way as the direct object pronouns we have seen in chapters 42 and 43.

Subject + IOP + verb
Subject + IOP + auxiliary + past participle

Here are the indirect object pronouns in French:

AUDIO 44.2 ◀))

<u>Singular</u>

me – m' – *me*
te – t' – *you*
lui – *him/her/it*

<u>Plural</u>

nous – *us*
vous – *you*
leur – *them*

Agreement of the Indirect Object Pronoun

Indirect object pronouns don't agree in gender and number with the past participle. The verb doesn't change when an indirect object pronoun is placed before the verb. Much easier than direct object pronouns!

En regardant la traduction, ajoutez **le bon pronom indirect** à la phrase.
By looking at the translation, add the right indirect pronoun to the sentence.

1. Il _____ a acheté un collier quand il était en vacances.
   He bought me a necklace when he was on vacation.

2. Ce costume _____ va très bien.
   This suit suits you very well. (singular)

3. Est-ce que je peux _____ demander quelque chose ?
   Can I ask you something? (plural)

4. Il _____ a dit qu'il allait vendre sa maison.
   He told us he was going to sell his house.

5. Est-ce que tu _____ as écrit cette année ?
   Did you write to her this year?

6. On _____ a envoyé leurs cadeaux d'anniversaire.
   We sent them their birthday presents.

7. Il _____ a répondu hier soir.
   He responded to us last night.

8. Fais attention, tu vas _____ faire mal.
   Be careful, you'll hurt him.

9. J'espère qu'il va _____ pardonner.
   I hope he will forgive me.

10. Est-ce qu'il _____ a parlé de son nouveau projet ?
    Has he told you about his new project? (plural)

11. Je _____ promets de venir à ton spectacle.
    I promise to come to your show. (singular)

12. Il _____ a raconté une histoire avant de dormir.
    He told them a bedtime story.

13. Plus tu grandis, plus tu   ressembles.

The older you get, the more you look like her.

14. Le vétérinaire   a téléphoné pour   rappeler l'opération de mon chien.

The vet called me to remind me of my dog's operation.

15. Ce n'est pas moi qui   ai volé son argent.

It wasn't me who stole his money.

LES PRONOMS Y ET EN

THE PRONOUNS Y AND EN

Y and **en** are common French pronouns used to replace places, things and quantities. In this lesson, we are going to focus on when **Y** and **EN** replace prepositions and partitive articles.

The Pronoun Y

Y will replace a part of the sentence indicating a place starting with one of the following prepositions.

AUDIO 45.1 ◄))

à – *to/at*

Je vais <u>à Paris</u>.	**J'<u>y</u> vais.**
I go to Paris.	*I go (there).*

en – *to*

Tu es <u>en Belgique</u>.	**Tu <u>y</u> es.**
You are in Belgium.	*You're there.*

dans – *in*

Il est <u>dans la voiture</u>.	**Il <u>y</u> est.**
He's in the car.	*He is there.*

chez – *at someone's place*

Elle est <u>chez le dentiste</u>.	**Elle <u>y</u> est.**
She's at the dentist.	*She's there.*

The Preposition à

For things, we will mostly use **Y** to replace a noun introduced by **the preposition à**, so **à** – **au** – **aux** – **à l'** – **à la**. Things can be physical or not, as well as places.

Je me fie <u>à mon intuition</u>.	**Je m'<u>y</u> fie.**
I trust my intuition.	*I trust it.*

The Pronoun EN

En also replaces a part of the sentence, including **the preposition de** and **partitive articles**, so **de – du – de l' – de la – des**.

AUDIO 45.2 ◄))

J'ai de la farine.	**J'en ai.**
I have flour.	*I have some.*

Where to Place Y and EN

Like most pronouns in French, they will be placed before the verb and the auxiliary for compound tenses.

Subject + y/en + verb
Subject + y/en + auxiliary + past participle

Subject + n' + y/en + verb + pas
Subject + n' + y/en + auxiliary + pas + past participle

AUDIO 45.3 ◄))

Réécrivez la phrase en remplaçant le groupe de mots par **y** ou **en**.
Rewrite the sentence by replacing the group of words with y or en.

1. Est-ce que tu es déjà allé **à Disneyland** ?
   Have you ever been to Disneyland?

2. On a décidé de ne pas aller **au cinéma** ce soir.
   We decided not to go to the cinema tonight.

3. Est-ce que vous avez besoin **d'argent** ?
   Do you need money?

4. Je vais **à la boulangerie** sur le chemin du travail.
   I go to the bakery on the way to work.

5. Il travaille **au centre-ville**.
   He works downtown.

6. Tu bois **du café** ?
   Do you drink coffee?

7. J'ai acheté un bouquet de fleurs **au marché**.
   I bought a bouquet of flowers at the market.

8. Il y a **de l'eau** dans son bol.
   There is water in his bowl.

9. Tu as pris le train pour aller **à Lisbonne** ?
   Did you take the train to go to Lisbon?

10. On mange **des pommes de terre** plusieurs fois par semaine.
    We eat potatoes several times a week.

11. Est-ce que tu es sûr **de cette réponse** ?
    Are you sure about this answer?

12. Tu vas **à la plage** demain matin ?
    Are you going to the beach tomorrow morning?

13. Qu'est-ce que tu penses **de mon pull** ?
    They have been living in this apartment for a few years.

14. Elles habitent **dans cet appartement** depuis quelques années.
    What do you think of my sweater?

15. Elle a hérité **de cette maison**.
    She inherited this house.

LES PRONOMS TONIQUES
EMPHATIC PRONOUNS

> **Emphatic pronouns**, also called stress pronouns, or **pronoms toniques** in French, are used to emphasize, to put the accent on a person. They are only used for people.

French Emphatic Pronouns

AUDIO 46.1 ◀))

<u>Singular</u>

moi – *me*
toi – *you*
lui – *him*
elle – *her*

<u>Plural</u>

nous – *us*
vous – *you*
eux – *them (m)*
elles – *them (f)*
soi – *oneself*

We use emphatic pronouns in many sentence structures:

AUDIO 46.2 ◀))

On their own or with an adverb

Qui a mangé le dernier croissant ?   <u>Moi.</u>
Who ate the last croissant?   *Me.*

After prepositions such as **avec** *(with)*, **pour** *(for)*, **sans** *(without)*, **chez** *(at someone's house)*

Tu veux venir avec <u>nous</u> ?
Do you want to come with us?

After **à** and **de**

On n'a pas peur de <u>toi</u>.
We're not afraid of you.

With comparisons

Il est plus grand qu'<u>elle</u>.
He is taller than her.

With **ne ... que**

On ne regarde que <u>lui</u>.
We only look at him.

To emphasize

<u>Vous</u>, vous êtes toujours à l'heure.
You are always on time.

When the subject is made out of a pronoun and a noun, or two pronouns

Mes parents et <u>moi</u> allons en vacances bientôt.
My parents and I are going on vacation soon.

After **c'est** and **ce sont**

C'est <u>toi</u> qui as appelé ?
Did you call?

 Ajoutez **un pronom tonique** à la phrase en vous aidant de la traduction.
Add an emphatic pronoun to the sentence using the translation as help.

1. Tu veux venir avec _____ au cinéma ?
   Do you want to come with us to the cinema?

2. Ce colis vient d'arriver. Je pense que c'est pour _____ .
   This package has just arrived. I think it's for you. (plural)

3. Elle est toujours fière de _____ .
   She is always proud of me.

4. Tu te souviens d'_____ ?
   Do you remember them? (masculine)

5. Mon frère est aussi grand que _____ .
   My brother is as tall as you. (singular)

6. _____ , ils ne me parlent jamais.
   They never talk to me.

7. Tyler et _____ sont amis depuis qu'ils sont petits.
   Tyler and him have been friends since they were little.

8. C'est _____ qui viens de m'appeler ?
   Was it you who just called me? (singular)

9. _____ , je ne l'aime pas beaucoup.
    I don't like him very much.

10. Ce portefeuille est à _____ .
    This wallet is mine.

11. Elle vient cet après-midi pour passer du temps avec _____ .
    She is coming this afternoon to spend time with us.

12. J'ai eu de meilleures notes qu'_____ .
    I got better grades than them. (feminine)

13. On l'a attendue mais on est partis sans _____ .
    We waited for her, but we left without her.

14. _____ , je n'ai pas envie d'y aller.
    I don't feel like going.

15. Est-ce que ce livre est à _____ ou à _____ ?
    Is this book yours or his? (singular)

QUI OU QUE
QUI OR QUE

47

Relative pronouns, **les pronoms relatifs** in French, link the main clause to the relative clause. French has 5 relative pronouns: **que – qui – dont – où – lequel**, but in this lesson, we are going to focus on **qui** and **que**.

Qui

Qui replaces <u>the subject</u> and can be translated to *who*, *which*, or *that*. The subject can be a person or a thing. **Qui** can never be **qu'** in front of a vowel.

→ Use **qui** when followed by a verb or a pronoun (reflexive pronoun – direct object pronoun – indirect object pronoun)

French reflexive pronouns
me – te – se – nous – vous – se

French direct object pronouns
me – te – le – la – nous – vous – les

French indirect object pronouns
me – te – lui – nous – vous – leur

AUDIO 47.1 ◄))

Je connais quelqu'un <u>qui</u> habite ici.
I know someone who lives here.

Que

Que replaces <u>the direct object</u> and can be translated to *who*, *whom*, *which*, or *that*.
Que becomes **qu'** when placed before a word starting with a vowel or a silent h.

→ **Que** is always followed by a subject pronoun or a noun, but not a verb.

French subject pronouns
Je – Tu – Il – Elle – On – Nous – Vous – Ils – Elles

AUDIO 47.2 ◄))

C'est le livre <u>que</u> j'ai lu.
It's the book that I read.

Ajoutez **qui** ou **que/qu'** à chaque phrase.
Add qui or que/qu' to each sentence.

1. Mon ami _____ sera là ce soir, vient de perdre son travail.
   My friend who will be here tonight just lost his job.

2. Elle a adoré le cadeau _____ tu lui as acheté.
   She loved the gift that you bought her.

3. C'est toi _____ m'as appelé ?
   Was it you who called me?

4. _____ est là ?
   Who's there?

5. J'ai trouvé la boucle d'oreille _____ j'avais perdue.
   I found the earring that I lost.

6. Le film _____ on a regardé hier soir n'était pas terrible.
   The movie we watched last night wasn't great.

7. Tu connais déjà mes amis _____ seront à la fête.
   You already know my friends who will be at the party.

8. C'est ce _____ j'ai dit.
   That's what I said.

9. On a réservé une place dans le train _____ part à deux heures.
   We booked a seat on the train that leaves at two o'clock.

10. Voilà le document _____ tu m'as demandé.
    Here's the document you asked me for.

11. Le chien _____ aboie est le chien des voisins.
    The barking dog is the neighbors' dog.

12. J'ai finalement trouvé les clés _____ j'avais perdues.
    I finally found the keys that I had lost.

13. On est allés au restaurant _____ tu nous as recommandé.

We went to the restaurant that you recommended to us.

14. Tu entends les oiseaux _____ chantent ?

Can you hear the birds singing?

15. C'est elle _____ est toujours en retard, pas moi.

It's her who is always late, not me.

IL FAUT QUE + SUBJONCTIF
IL FAUT QUE + SUBJUNCTIVE

> **Il faut que** is a French impersonal expression used to say *To have to*. The tricky part is that this impersonal expression is followed by the French subjunctive, always, no exceptions!

In this exercise, we are going to focus on the 3 groups of regular verbs.

How to Build the Subjunctive

The **subjonctif présent** is formed by taking the verb conjugated in the present tense with **ils** and removing the **-ent**. That gives us the stem. Then we add the endings for the subjonctif présent: **-e, -es, -e, -ions, iez** and **-ent**.

Chercher – *To search*	**Finir** – *To finish*	**Attendre** – *To wait*
AUDIO 48.1 ◀	AUDIO 48.2 ◀	AUDIO 48.3 ◀
Ils cherch**ent**	Ils finiss**ent**	Ils attend**ent**
Stem: cherch	Stem: finiss	Stem: attend
Que je cherche	**Que je finisse**	**Que j'attende**
Que tu cherches	**Que tu finisses**	**Que tu attendes**
Qu'il-Qu'elle-Qu'on cherche	**Qu'il-Qu'elle-Qu'on finisse**	**Qu'il-Qu'elle-Qu'on attende**
Que nous cherchions	**Que nous finissions**	**Que nous attendions**
Que vous cherchiez	**Que vous finissiez**	**Que vous attendiez**
Qu'ils-Qu'elles cherchent	**Qu'ils-Qu'elles finissent**	**Qu'ils-Qu'elles attendent**

AUDIO 48.4 ◀

Reflexive verbs are conjugated the same way: **Il faut que je <u>me lave</u>** – *I have to shower.*

AUDIO 48.5 ◀

 Conjuguez le verbe donné au **subjonctif**. <u>Acheter</u> change d'accent avec la conjugaison.
Conjugate the given verb in the subjunctive. Acheter has a change in accent with the conjugation.

1. **travailler** – Il faut que nous _____ moins.

   We need to work less.

---

2. **nourrir** – Il faut que tu   le bébé.

   You have to feed the baby.

3. **acheter** – Il faut qu'elle   ses billets d'avion avant qu'ils soient trop chers.

   She needs to buy her plane tickets before they are too expensive.

4. **attendre** – Il faut que j'   mon mari pour partir.

   I have to wait for my husband to leave.

5. **tondre** – Il faut qu'il   la pelouse.

   He has to mow the lawn.

6. **ranger** – Il faut que je   ma chambre.

   I have to tidy my room.

7. **agir** – Il faut qu'on   au plus vite.

   We need to act as quickly as possible.

8. **trouver** – Il faut que tu   une solution.

   You have to find a solution.

9. **réussir** – Il faut que vous   vos examens.

   You must pass your exams.

10. **économiser** – Il faut que nous   plus.

    We need to save more.

11. **étudier** – Il faut que j'   pour mes examens.

    I have to study for my exams.

12. **arrêter** – Il faut qu'ils   de fumer.

    They need to stop smoking.

13. **marcher** – Il faut que tu   plus vite.

    You need to walk faster.

14. **parler** – Il faut qu'elle   à son patron de son idée.

    She needs to talk to her boss about her idea.

15. **vendre** – Il faut que je   cette maison.

    I have to sell this house.

PLACEZ LE MOT AU BON ENDROIT
PLACE THE WORD IN THE RIGHT SPOT

49

A little challenge for you with a missing word. Technically, not missing, because I give it to you, but you have to find the right spot for it in the sentence.

AUDIO 49.1 ◀ɔ)

 Réécrivez la phrase et ajoutez le mot au bon endroit.
Rewrite the sentence and add the word in the right spot.

1. **intéressant** – Je lis un article dans le journal.

   I am reading an interesting article in the newspaper.

2. **fois** – Elle perd ses écouteurs deux par jour.

   She loses her headphones twice a day.

3. **de** – Le mari ma tante est mon oncle.

   My aunt's husband is my uncle.

4. **grande** – Ma sœur est née en janvier.

   My big sister was born in January.

5. **tellement** – Ce chien est adorable !

   This dog is so adorable!

6. **honte** – J'ai de mes résultats.

   I am ashamed of my results.

7. **après** – N'oublie pas de te brosser les dents.

   Don't forget to brush your teeth afterwards.

8. **blancs** – Ma grand-mère a de plus en plus de cheveux.

   My grandmother has more and more white hair.

9. **jamais** – Il ne porte son alliance.

   He never wears his wedding ring.

10. **ça** – C'est facile pour toi de dire.

    It's easy for you to say that.

11. **trop** – Ce film est beaucoup long !

    This movie is way too long!

12. **nouveaux** – On a acheté nos bijoux à la bijouterie.

    We bought our new jewelry at the jewelry store.

13. **petit** – Mes voisins ont adopté un garçon.

    My neighbors adopted a little boy.

14. **toujours** – Je prends une douche le soir.

    I always take a shower in the evening.

15. **salé** – Ce plat est trop pour moi.

    This dish is too salty for me.

35 QUESTIONS

35 QUESTIONS

50

This is already the last chapter of the book. I hope all the chapters gave you a chance to learn or review the rules I have selected for you. Let's do one final exercise using everything we learned from the book.

AUDIO 50.1 🔊

 Choisissez entre **les deux réponses** possibles pour chaque question.
Choose between the two possible answers for each question.

1. **un – une** – Je viens de voir   étoile filante.
   I just saw a shooting star.

2. **clous – cloux** – Sa boîte de   est tombée de l'étagère.
   His box of nails fell off the shelf.

3. **architect – architecte** – L'   a approuvé les plans finaux.
   The architect approved the final plans.

4. **espagnole – espagnol** – Ma femme est   .
   My wlfe is Spanish.

5. **était – sera** – On   au marché ce samedi pour vendre nos légumes.
   We will be at the market this Saturday to sell our vegetables.

6. **Ils – Elles** – Ce sont Julie et Laura.   sont cousines.
   They are Julie and Laura. They are cousins.

7. **le – la** – J'ai mis   journal sur la table pour toi.
   I put the newspaper on the table for you.

8. **s'habille – m'habille** – Je   toujours après mon petit déjeuner.
   I always get dressed after my breakfast.

9. **réveille – se réveille** – Elle   les enfants tous les jours à 7 heures.
   She wakes up the children every day at 7 a.m.

10. **sa** – **la** – Il se rase _____ moustache une ou deux fois par semaine.
    He shaves his mustache once or twice a week.

11. **cette** – **ce** – Est-ce que tu as vu _____ promotion ?
    Have you seen this sale?

12. **aurais** – **aurai** – J' _____ plus de temps pour moi si je travaillais moins.
    I would have more time for myself if I worked less.

13. **avoir** – **être** – Tu ne devrais pas _____ honte de ton travail.
    You shouldn't be ashamed of your work.

14. **ma** – **mon** – J'ai pris _____ anorak mais je l'ai laissé dans la voiture.
    I took my rain jacket but left it in the car.

15. **ces** – **ses** – Tu sais à qui sont _____ chaussures ?
    Do you know whose shoes these are?

16. **Leur** – **Leurs** – _____ idée était bonne mais pas géniale.
    Their idea was good, but not great.

17. **Vingt-et-un** – **Vingt et un** – _____ joueurs participent à la compétition.
    Twenty-one players participate in the competition.

18. **a** – **est** – Il _____ descendu le tableau au garage.
    He took the board down to the garage.

19. **été** – **eu** – J'ai _____ beaucoup de chance quand j'ai acheté ma maison.
    I was very lucky when I bought my house.

20. **étudier** – **étudié** – Il a toujours besoin de calme pour _____ .
    He always needs quiet time to study.

21. **à la** – **au** – Demande _____ caissier de te donner un sac en papier.
    Ask the cashier to give you a paper bag.

22. **du** – **de** – Je me souviens _____ vieux bâtiment qui a été détruit.
    I remember the old building that was destroyed.

23. **à – de** – Tu as tort   ne pas faire attention à ton argent.

You are wrong for not being careful with your money.

24. **au – en** – On sera   Grèce à la fin de la semaine.

We will be in Greece at the end of the week.

25. **apprennes – apprends** – Il faut que tu   ta leçon.

You have to learn your lesson.

26. **Quel – Quelle** –   est ta série préférée ?

What is your favorite TV show?

27. **faux – fausses** – Je pense que ces réponses sont   .

I think these answers are wrong.

28. **vieil – vieux** – Le   ascenseur de notre immeuble est toujours en panne.

The old elevator in our building is still broken.

29. **superstitieux – superstitieuse** – Est-ce qu'il est   ?

Is he superstitious?

30. **était – étaient** – On   proches avant de vivre dans différentes villes.

We were close before living in different cities.

31. **à la – au** – Je ne sais pas ce que j'ai fait mais j'ai mal   poignet.

I don't know what I did but my wrist hurts.

32. **feras – ferais** – Tu   la lessive quand tu rentres ?

Will you do the laundry when you get home?

33. **vient – a** – Elle   de recevoir son diplôme.

She has just received her diploma.

34. **tu – toi** – Cet appartement est parfait pour   !

This apartment is perfect for you!

35. **qui – que** – Ce n'est pas la chanson   j'ai entendue.

This is not the song I heard.

ANSWER KEY

1. Est-ce que tu veux **un** café ?
2. Elle a **une** bonne idée pour ton cadeau d'anniversaire.
3. Mes parents travaillent dans **un** magasin de décoration.
4. C'est important d'avoir **une** chambre propre.
5. On a planté **des** arbres pour avoir un peu d'ombre dans le jardin.
6. Il y a **des** oranges sur la table.
7. Casser **un** miroir porte malheur.
8. C'est **une** idée géniale !
9. Je pense qu'elle a **un** nouveau téléphone.
10. Il y a **des** croissants pour le petit déjeuner.
11. On a reçu **une** invitation mais ce n'est pas pour nous.
12. J'habite dans **un** petit appartement.
13. Cette voiture a **des** options intéressantes.
14. Il y a **une** personne dans la salle d'attente.
15. N'oublie pas de faire **un** vœu !

CHAPTER 2

1. On va jouer à des **jeux** de société ce soir.
2. La laine est pleine de **nœuds**.
3. Certains **animaux** sont en danger d'extinction.
4. J'ai deux **chiens** et deux **chats**.
5. Les **oiseaux** attendent que je lance des **graines**.
6. Je ne trouve pas les **clous** pour réparer le plancher.
7. Il y a trop de **choix**.
8. Ces **clients** ont réservé la salle numéro 3.
9. J'aime écouter des **chansons** quand je travaille.
10. Ça fait toujours plaisir de recevoir des **fleurs**.
11. Les **repas** sont servis à dix-neuf heures.
12. Il a perdu beaucoup de **cheveux**.
13. On utilise des **journaux** pour commencer le feu.
14. Les **bocaux** ne sont pas propres.
15. Est-ce que tu as lu ces **romans** ?

CHAPTER 3

1. Un **facteur** – Une factrice livre le courrier et les colis.
2. Un opticien – Une **opticienne** vérifie la vue de ses clients.
3. Un **boulanger** – Une boulangère prépare des pains et des pâtisseries.
4. Un enseignant – Une **enseignante** donne des cours aux enfants.
5. Un **infirmier** – Une infirmière prodigue des soins aux patients.
6. Un guide – Une **guide** accompagne les touristes.
7. Un **magicien** – Une magicienne réalise des tours de magie.
8. Un éducateur – Une **éducatrice** travaille avec des enfants ou des adultes.
9. Un **reporteur** – Une reportrice récolte des informations et réalise des interviews.
10. Un secrétaire – Une **secrétaire** accomplit les tâches administratives.
11. Un **dentiste** – Une dentiste traite les problèmes dentaires.
12. Un avocat – Une **avocate** représente ses clients au tribunal.
13. Un **pharmacien** – Une pharmacienne prépare et vend des médicaments.
14. Un acteur – Une **actrice** joue des rôles pour des films ou des séries.
15. Un **étudiant** – Une étudiante va à l'école tous les jours.

CHAPTER 4

1. Cédric est **français**, il vient de **France**.
2. Sarah est **algérienne**, elle vient d'**Algérie**.
3. Mon père est **sénégalais**, il vient du **Sénégal**.
4. Tu es **belge**, tu viens de **Belgique**.
5. Son professeur est **italien**, il vient d'**Italie**.
6. Ma colocataire est **irlandaise**, elle vient d'**Irlande**.
7. Mon collègue est **suisse**, il vient de **Suisse**.
8. Mon amie est **japonaise**, elle vient du **Japon**.
9. Lisa est **canadienne**, elle vient du **Canada**.
10. Mon patron est **vietnamien**, il vient du **Vietnam**.
11. Jeff est **marocain**, il vient du **Maroc**.
12. Pedro est **portugais**, il vient du **Portugal**.
13. Nora est **indienne**, elle vient d'**Inde**.
14. Cet auteur est **philippin**, il vient des **Philippines**.
15. Le maire est **luxembourgeois**, il vient du **Luxembourg**.

CHAPTER 5

1. **Julie et Anthony** sont dans la même classe.
   Ils sont dans la même classe.

2. **La souris** est sur le bureau.
   Elle est sur le bureau.

3. **Le ciel** est couvert ce matin.
   Il est couvert ce matin.

4. **Mon passeport** est dans le coffre-fort.
   Il est dans le coffre-fort.

5. **Flore et moi** serons en congé en même temps.
   Nous serons en congé en même temps.

6. Attention, **la poêle** est très chaude.
   Attention, **elle** est très chaude.

7. **Ton frère et toi** devriez regarder ce film.
   Vous devriez regarder ce film.

8. **La piscine** sera fermée samedi.
   Elle sera fermée samedi.

9. Malheureusement, **mon fils** n'a pas réussi son permis de conduire.
   Malheureusement, **il** n'a pas réussi son permis de conduire.

10. **Ma voisine** sera à la retraite dans quelques mois.
    Elle sera à la retraite dans quelques mois.

11. **Le lait** est périmé.
    Il est périmé.

12. **Sa montre** est en panne pour la deuxième fois.
    Elle est en panne pour la deuxième fois.

13. **Lina et Pascal** sont allergiques aux œufs.
    Ils sont allergiques aux œufs.

14. **Mon professeur** est vraiment passionné par son travail.

Il est vraiment passionné par son travail.

15. **La tempête** a déjà commencé.

Elle a déjà commencé.

CHAPTER 6

1. Présent de l'indicatif : Je **suis** étudiant.
2. Imparfait x2 : Quand on **était** jeunes, on **était** timides.
3. Futur simple : Demain, il **sera** à Paris pour son concert.
4. Passé composé : J'**ai été** malade après le repas.
5. Impératif : **Sois** prudent quand tu conduis !
6. Conditionnel présent : Je ne sais pas si je **serais** plus heureux avec plus d'argent.
7. Subjonctif présent : Il faut que tu **sois** là pour signer les documents.
8. Imparfait : Si tu **étais** ici, tu comprendrais.
9. Passé récent : Je **viens d'être** élu maire de la ville.
10. Futur proche : Elle **va être** diplômée dans quelques semaines.
11. Passé composé : Elle **a été** surprise par le résultat du match.
12. Imparfait – Conditionnel présent : Si j'**étais** toi, je **serais** plus attentif pendant les cours.
13. Futur simple : Demain, nous **serons** enfin en vacances.
14. Présent de l'indicatif : Pourquoi est-ce que tu n'**es** pas d'accord ?
15. Conditionnel présent : Tu ne **serais** pas en retard si tu t'étais réveillé à l'heure.

CHAPTER 7

1. Il travaille seul, il n'a pas **de** collègues.

→ In a negative sentence, **des** changes to **de**.

2. **Les enfants** ont un anniversaire ce samedi.

→ The plural of **enfant** is **enfants**.

3. Je pense qu'il est **canadien** mais je ne suis pas certaine.

→ **Il** is masculine so the nationality should be **canadien**.

4. Le client n'est pas content. **Il** dit que les légumes ne sont pas frais.

→ **Le client** is masculine singular. The right subject pronoun is **il**.

5. Elle mange une pomme et **une** poire.

   → Here the second **une** is missing before **poire**.

6. Il s'est fait mal aux **genoux**.

   → The plural of **genou** is **genoux**.

7. Le **vétérinaire** soigne les animaux.

   → **Vétérinaire** always takes an **-e** at the end.

8. Marie est **française** mais elle habite aux États-Unis.

   → **français** should be feminine because Marie is a woman, so **française**.

9. J'ai bu **un** café après le repas.

   → **Café** is masculine so the article should be **un**.

10. J'attends un appel de mon **avocate**.

    → The feminine of **avocat** is **avocate**.

11. Il faut qu'on **soit** prêts pour la réception.

    → The verb **être** in the **subjonctif** with **on** is **soit**.

12. **Je** viens juste de partir.

    → Before a word starting with a consonant, use **Je**, not **J'**.

13. Les **prix** augmentent constamment.

    → The plural of **prix** stays **prix**.

14. Est-ce que tu es déjà allé en **Inde** ?

    → **Inde** is a country and starts with a capital letter.

15. Je ne **serai** pas là quand tu arrives.

    → **Être** conjugated in the **futur simple** with **Je** is **serai**.

CHAPTER 8

1. Je n'ai pas enregistré **le** document avant de fermer l'ordinateur.

2. Est-ce que tu as goûté **le** pain ?

3. **Le** pays traverse une situation économique difficile.

4. Elle fait tremper **les** pois chiches pendant des heures.

5. **Le/La** ministre a un rendez-vous avec **les** journalistes.

6. **La** crise a été évitée de peu.

7. Parfois, on peut voir **le** raton laveur qui vit dans **le** jardin.

8. Il adore **la** mode.

9. **L'**année a été difficile pour **les** fermiers.

10. **Le** jour où tu es né était **le** plus beau jour de ma vie.

11. **Le** prix va diminuer dans **les** prochains jours.

12. Tu te souviens de **la** fois où il est tombé dans **les** escaliers ?

13. **L'**homme que j'ai vu ne ressemblait pas à ce portrait.

14. **Le** chien des voisins se sauve souvent.

15. **La** question qu'il a posée est une bonne question.

CHAPTER 9

1. Il y a **un** avion dans **le** ciel.

2. J'ai commandé **le** livre dont tu m'as parlé.

3. Est-ce que tu veux regarder **un** film ce soir ?

4. Je suis certaine que **la** voiture que j'ai vue était noire.

5. Il y a **des** oiseaux qui chantent dans **l'**arbre.

6. **Les** fleurs de ton jardin sont magnifiques.

7. **La** femme que j'ai rencontrée au supermarché était très gentille.

8. **Les** étoiles brillent pendant **la** nuit.

9. **Une** de mes amies vient de se marier.

10. Mon chien aboie après **une** souris.

11. On a vu **un** ours durant notre voyage au Canada.

12. **Les** clients font **la** queue pour attendre leur tour.

13. J'ai envie de faire **une** sieste.

14. Est-ce que tu as **le** temps de discuter un peu ?

15. **L'**appartement se trouve au deuxième étage.

CHAPTER 10

1. **Se demander** – Je **me demande** comment il va.

2. **S'excuser** – Il **s'excuse** toujours trop tard.

3. **S'amuser** – Les enfants **s'amusent** dans le jardin.

4. **Se maquiller** – Elle **se maquille** avant de s'habiller.

5. **Se promener** – Les touristes **se promènent** toujours dans cette partie de la ville.
6. **Se réveiller** – On **se réveille** tous les jours à 6 heures.
7. **Se préparer** – Ils **se préparent** pour sortir.
8. **Se laver** – Je **me lave** le soir au lieu du matin.
9. **Se marier** – Ils **se marient** ce matin à la mairie.
10. **S'habiller** – Mon fils **s'habille** seul depuis quelques temps.
11. **Se comporter** – Le chien **se comporte** bizarrement.
12. **Se brosser** – Je **me brosse** les dents trois fois par jour.
13. **Se reposer** – Mon père **se repose** dans le canapé.
14. **S'adapter** – Ma fille **s'adapte** assez vite à sa nouvelle école.
15. **S'habituer** – Je **m'habitue** doucement à mon nouvel appareil dentaire.

CHAPTER 11

1. Promener – ~~Se promener~~ – On **promène** le chien au parc.
2. ~~Maquiller~~ – Se maquiller – Est-ce que tu **te maquilles** tous les jours ?
3. ~~Appeler~~ – S'appeler – Je **m'appelle** Dylane, et toi ?
4. Demander – ~~Se demander~~ – L'élève **demande** de l'aide au professeur.
5. ~~Épiler~~ – S'épiler – Je ne **m'épile** pas toutes les semaines.
6. Couper – ~~Se couper~~ – Elle **coupe** les légumes pour le dîner.
7. ~~Perdre~~ – Se perdre – On **se perd** toujours quand on voyage.
8. Tromper – ~~Se tromper~~ – Je ne le savais pas mais il **trompe** sa femme.
9. Appuyer – ~~S'appuyer~~ – Le petit garçon **appuie** sur le bouton de l'ascenseur.
10. Rappeler – ~~Se rappeler~~ – Je **rappelle** ce client tout de suite.
11. Sécher – ~~Se sécher~~ – Le linge **sèche** dans le jardin.
12. ~~Changer~~ – Se changer – Je **me change** car mon pull est taché.
13. ~~Inquiéter~~ – S'inquiéter – Elle **s'inquiète** beaucoup pour son avenir.
14. Conduire – ~~Se conduire~~ – Ma voisine **conduit** son mari au travail tous les jours.
15. ~~Asseoir~~ – S'asseoir – Ça va pour toi si on **s'assoit** ici ?

CHAPTER 12

1. Il se rase **la** barbe tous les jours.
2. Est-ce te tu t'es peigné **les** cheveux ?
3. Il faut se laver **les** mains plusieurs fois par jour.
4. N'oublie pas de te sécher **les** cheveux.
5. Elle s'est cassé **le** pied il y a plusieurs années.

6. Je dois me limer **les** ongles mais je ne trouve pas ma lime.

7. Une personne s'est foulé **la** cheville en sortant du restaurant.

8. C'est important de se brosser **les** cheveux tous les jours.

9. Merci de vous essuyer **les** pieds.

10. Je n'ai pas toujours le temps de m'épiler **les** sourcils.

CHAPTER 13

1. **Cette** robe est superbe. Elle te va très bien.

2. Tu as vu **ce** nouvel article dans le journal ?

3. **Ces** fleurs sentent vraiment bon.

4. **Cet** exercice est un peu trop facile pour moi.

5. C'est **cette** voiture que je voulais acheter.

6. **Cet** appartement est trop petit pour nous.

7. Est-ce que **ce** stylo est à toi ?

8. **Cet** homme ressemble beaucoup à mon père.

9. **Cette** montagne est dangereuse pour les skieurs.

10. Fais attention, **ce** café est très chaud.

11. J'ai beaucoup aimé **cette** chanson.

12. **Cet** ordinateur tombe toujours en panne.

13. **Cette** chaise n'est pas confortable du tout.

14. Beaucoup de gens se perdent dans **ce** parc.

15. **Ces** plantes que tu as achetées sont magnifiques.

CHAPTER 14

1. Présent : J'**ai** un chien et deux chats.

2. Futur simple : Demain, on **aura** nos résultats.

3. Passé composé : Hier, elle **a eu** une idée de génie.

4. Impératif : **Aie** confiance en toi !

5. Futur simple : Mes parents **auront** leur nouvelle voiture quand on les verra.

6. Subjonctif présent : Il faut que tu **aies** plus de points pour réussir.

7. Présent : Le secrétaire **a** le temps de remplir les documents.

8. Imparfait : J'**avais** un vélo comme celui-ci quand j'étais petite.

9. Passé composé : Il **a eu** ce qu'il voulait.

10. Passé récent : Mon ami **vient d'avoir** son permis de conduire.

11. Subjonctif présent : Il faut que le passager **ait** son billet pour monter dans l'avion.

12. Futur simple : Demain, nous **aurons** finalement les clés de notre nouvelle maison.

13. Présent : Est-ce que tu **as** un peu de temps pour moi ?

14. Futur proche : Mon frère et sa femme **vont avoir** un bébé dans les prochains jours.

15. Passé composé : Il **a eu** un accident de voiture hier soir mais il va bien.

CHAPTER 15

1. J'**ai** tellement faim !

2. Tu **es** né le même jour que moi.

3. Son sac à main **est** noir.

4. Mets un pull si tu **as** froid.

5. Je pense qu'il **est** prêt pour son examen.

6. On **a** hâte de partir en vacances.

7. Nous **sommes** en train de préparer le dîner.

8. Il **est** en route mais il sera en retard.

9. Elle **a** vraiment besoin de se reposer.

10. Mon oncle n'**est** pas en bonne santé.

11. J'**ai** mal aux dents mais je ne veux pas aller chez le dentiste.

12. Est-ce que tu **as** peur du noir ?

13. Elle **est** de bonne humeur aujourd'hui.

14. J'**ai** toujours de la chance quand je joue à la loterie.

15. C'**est** une personne très gentille.

CHAPTER 16

1. Est-ce que c'est **ton** livre sur la table ?

2. **Sa** maison est vraiment jolie mais elle est un peu grande.

3. **Tes** lunettes sont de travers.

4. Comment se sont passées **ses** vacances ?

5. Tous **mes** rendez-vous ont été annulés.

6. Fais **tes** devoirs avant d'aller jouer.

7. **Mon** école va être rénovée pendant les vacances d'été.

8. Est-ce que **ta** voiture est finalement réparée ?

9. Il laisse toujours **ses** jouets partout dans la maison.

10. **Ma** mère ne pourra pas être là à la remise des clés.

11. Elle a encore oublié **son** sac dans le train.

12. **Tes** cours commencent à quelle heure ?

13. **Son** ordinateur est branché mais il ne s'allume pas.

14. **Mes** habits sont toujours dans le sèche-linge.

15. **Ton** horaire est affiché dans la classe.

CHAPTER 17

1. Qui a peint **ces** peintures ?

2. **Ses** enfants ne regardent jamais la télévision.

3. Est-ce que tu as vu **ces** articles dans le journal ?

4. Qu'est-ce que vous pensez de **ses** idées ?

5. Est-ce que tu veux goûter un de **ces** macarons ?

6. Qu'est-ce que **ces** personnes sont devenues ?

7. **Ses** chaussures sont des chaussures de marque.

8. Tu as pensé à appeler **ces** clients ?

9. Elle a encadré **ses** photos préférées.

10. **Ces** maisons ont été rénovées récemment.

11. **Ces** lunettes sont à elle.

12. **Ses** nouveaux meubles sont plus modernes que les anciens.

13. Il a accueilli **ses** premiers clients ce matin.

14. Quel est le nom de **ces** montagnes ?

15. Il perd toujours **ses** affaires !

CHAPTER 18

1. **Nos** amis viennent nous rendre visite ce soir.

2. **Vos** chiens n'obéissent pas beaucoup.

3. **Nos** enfants vont à l'école ensemble.

4. **Leur** anniversaire de mariage est le même jour que le nôtre.

5. **Notre** maison est située à une centaine de mètres de la plage.

6. **Leur** jardin est plein de fleurs.

7. Bien sûr que **votre** avis est important pour nous.

8. **Leur** nouvelle cuisine est équipée des derniers gadgets.

9. **Notre** projet de construction avance bien.

10. **Vos** rendez-vous sont prévus pour demain matin.

11. **Notre** nouvel appartement est beaucoup plus spacieux.

12. **Leur** chat se promène souvent dans le quartier.

13. **Notre** voyage en Europe est réservé pour le mois prochain.

14. Est-ce que **votre** nouvelle voiture est une voiture électrique ?

15. **Nos** voisins organisent toujours un barbecue en été.

CHAPTER 19

11 – Onze

19 – Dix-neuf

21 – Vingt et un

29 – Vingt-neuf

36 – Trente-six

47 – Quarante-sept

52 – Cinquante-deux

63 – Soixante-trois

72 – Soixante-douze

77 – Soixante-dix-sept

80 – Quatre-vingts

89 – Quatre-vingt-neuf

92 – Quatre-vingt-douze

99 – Quatre-vingt-dix-neuf

100 – Cent

CHAPTER 20

1. J'ai le temps de prendre un café.

   Je **n'**ai **pas** le temps de prendre un café.

2. Tu es en retard.

   Tu **n'**es **pas** en retard.

3. Vous voulez venir avec nous ?

   Vous **ne** voulez **pas** venir avec nous ?

4. Elle lit quelques chapitres avant de dormir.

   Elle **ne** lit **pas** quelques chapitres avant de dormir.

5. Mon père regarde les informations tous les soirs.

Mon père **ne** regarde **pas** les informations tous les soirs.

6. J'ai un chien qui s'appelle Max.

Je **n'**ai **pas** <u>de</u> chien qui s'appelle Max.

7. Elle sera là samedi.

Elle **ne** sera **pas** là samedi.

8. J'ai bien compris la question.

Je **n'**ai **pas** bien compris la question.

9. On a acheté une petite maison dans le sud de la France.

On **n'**a **pas** acheté <u>de</u> petite maison dans le sud de la France.

10. Il a fait des efforts ces derniers mois.

Il **n'**a **pas** fait **d'**efforts ces derniers mois.

11. Je porte des chaussures.

Je **ne** porte **pas** <u>de</u> chaussures.

12. Il fait beau ce matin.

Il **ne** fait **pas** beau ce matin.

13. Il manque une pièce dans ce jeu de société.

Il **ne** manque **pas** <u>de</u> pièce dans ce jeu de société.

14. J'ai vu mon patron au parc.

Je **n'**ai **pas** vu mon patron au parc.

15. Elle aime la musique classique.

Elle **n'**aime **pas** la musique classique.

CHAPTER 21

1. Il **est monté** dans l'ascenseur après moi. (**monter**)

2. On **a mangé** des pâtes pour le déjeuner. (**manger**)

3. Est-ce que tu **as vu** ce film ? (**voir**)

4. Il **est parti** il y a deux heures. (**partir**)

5. Elle **a pris** les décisions pour la réunion. (**prendre**)

6. Ma fille **a commencé** à marcher tard. (**commencer**)

7. La caissière **a oublié** de me donner le ticket. (**oublier**)

8. Il **a plu** hier. (**pleuvoir**)

9. Mes parents **sont venus** manger à la maison. (**venir**)

10. Ils **se sont mariés** le mois dernier. (**se marier**)

11. J'**ai bu** un café délicieux. (**boire**)

12. Elle **a agi** sans réfléchir. (**agir**)

13. Les ambulanciers **sont arrivés** tout de suite. (**arriver**)

14. Est-ce qu'ils **ont vendu** leur voiture ? (**vendre**)

15. Les enfants **ont fait** leurs devoirs dans le salon. (**faire**)

CHAPTER 22

1. Ils sont **restés** à la maison toute la journée. (**rester**)

2. La chanteuse a **chanté** l'hymne national. (**chanter**)

3. Est-ce que tu as bien **dormi** ? (**dormir**)

4. Le coureur a **marché** pour finir la course. (**marcher**)

5. J'ai **entendu** quelque chose de bizarre. (**entendre**)

6. Il a **conduit** ses enfants à l'aéroport. (**conduire**)

7. On a **adopté** un chien au refuge. (**adopter**)

8. J'ai **lu** ce livre mais je ne l'ai pas **aimé**. (**lire – aimer**)

9. Il n'est pas **venu** avec moi. (**venir**)

10. Elles se sont **préparées** ensemble ce matin. (**se préparer**)

11. Le technicien a **remplacé** le filtre. (**remplacer**)

12. Mon voisin a **reçu** mon colis par erreur. (**recevoir**)

13. Elle a **écrit** ses mémoires il y a quelques années. (**écrire**)

14. Qu'est-ce que tu as **choisi** ? (**choisir**)

15. On t'a **attendu** toute la soirée. (**attendre**)

CHAPTER 23

1. Le chien veut **jouer** à la balle. (joué / jouer)

2. Elle adore **danser**. (dansé / danser)

3. Qu'est-ce que tu as **fait** ? (fait / faire)

4. J'ai **acheté** de nouveaux produits pour **nettoyer**. (acheté / acheter – nettoyé / nettoyer)

5. Est-ce que tu as **réussi** ton examen ? (réussi / ~~réussir~~)

6. Il n'a pas **pensé** à **appeler** la police. (pensé / ~~penser~~ – ~~appelé~~ / appeler)

7. Je n'arrive pas à y **croire**. (~~cru~~ / croire)

8. Elle a **offert** des fleurs à sa mère. (offert / ~~offrir~~)

9. Les enfants ont **appris** à **compter** à l'école. (appris / ~~apprendre~~ – ~~compté~~ / compter)

10. Elle a **éteint** la lumière avant de **sortir**. (éteint / ~~éteindre~~ – ~~sorti~~ / sortir)

11. Je n'ai pas **pu venir** avec toi. (pu / ~~pouvoir~~ – ~~venu~~ / venir)

12. Ça m'a beaucoup **fait rire** (fait / ~~faire~~ – ~~ri~~ / rire)

13. Qu'est-ce qu'il est **devenu** ? (devenu / ~~devenir~~)

14. On a **accueilli** nos premiers clients. (accueilli / ~~accueillir~~)

15. Est-ce que vous avez **réfléchi** à **changer** de voiture ?
    (réfléchi / ~~réfléchir~~ – ~~changé~~ / changer)

CHAPTER 24

1. J'ai lu tous les livres de **cet** auteur.
    → Because **auteur** starts with a vowel and is masculine, we use **cet**.

2. **Son** amie va passer le week-end chez nous.
    → Because **amie** starts with a vowel, we use **son**.

3. **Leurs** chiens jouent au parc pendant qu'ils discutent.
    → We use **leurs** when the following noun is plural.

4. Il n'**a** jamais de chance !
    → *To be lucky* translates to **avoir de la chance** in French.

5. À quelle heure est-ce que tu **te** réveilles ?
    → *To wake up* is a reflexive verb in French = **se réveiller**.

6. **Le** manteau que j'ai commandé n'est pas encore arrivé.
    → **Manteau** is masculine singular so we use **le**.

7. Quel âge est-ce que tu vas **avoir** ?
    → The used tense is **futur proche** including **aller** conjugated in the present tense followed by **avoir**.

8. Je **me** sèche les mains.
    → *To dry (a body part)* is a reflexive verb in French = **se sécher**.

9. Est-ce que tu t'es brossé **les** cheveux ?

    → Body parts after a reflexive verb never use a possessive adjective.

10. On **avait** toujours du beau temps en été.

    → **Avoir** conjugated with **on** has an **-ait** ending.

11. Mon grand-père a **soixante-dix-neuf** ans.

    → There is always a dash between numbers (except ... et un).

12. Je n'ai pas fait **de** faute dans mon examen.

    → In a negative sentence, **une** changes to **de**.

13. Il **est** tombé en faisant du vélo.

    → **Tomber** is conjugated with **être** in the passé composé.

14. Tu n'as toujours pas **reçu** la lettre que je t'ai envoyée ?

    → The past participle of **recevoir** is **reçu**.

15. N'oublie pas de **débrancher** le fer à repasser quand tu as fini.

    → After **de**, the verb is always infinitive in French.

CHAPTER 25

1. Elle a pardonné **aux** voleurs.
2. Fais attention **à la** marche.
3. Je ne fais pas confiance **aux** personnes que je ne connais pas.
4. On s'intéresse **aux** plantes de notre jardin.
5. Elle a dit **au** coiffeur de couper ses cheveux courts.
6. Je dois répondre **au** message de mon frère.
7. Tu veux jouer **aux** cartes avec nous ?
8. Ce sac va très bien **au** mannequin.
9. Le docteur rend visite **aux** patients tous les matins.
10. On a téléphoné **à la** mairie mais personne n'a répondu.
11. Elle a donné son ticket **à l'**homme devant elle.
12. Il ne croit pas **au** Père Noël.
13. Je m'habitue **aux** températures assez vite.
14. Est-ce que tu as parlé **à l'**architecte ?
15. J'écris une lettre **aux** docteurs.

CHAPTER 26

1. Il a toujours eu peur **des** serpents.
2. On vient juste de partir **de l'**aéroport.
3. J'ai envie **du** chocolat que j'ai acheté hier.
4. Méfie-toi **des** voisins.
5. Elle a hérité **de la** maison de ses parents.
6. Il a profité **du** problème.
7. Je me sers **de la** friteuse de temps en temps.
8. Qu'est-ce que tu penses **du** film ?
9. Tu te souviens **de la** personne qui conduisait ?
10. Il s'agit **du** papier que j'ai perdu.
11. Les spectateurs rient **de la** blague.
12. Tu leur as parlé **des** vacances ?
13. On a besoin **du** journal que je t'ai donné hier.
14. Les invités arrivent **du** mariage.
15. Elle se plaint toujours **de la** température.

CHAPTER 27

1. Il a choisi **de** vendre son entreprise l'année dernière.
2. Est-ce que tu peux m'aider **à** préparer le repas ?
3. Mon fils rêve **de** devenir astronaute.
4. J'ai appris **à** jouer de la guitare quand j'étais petite.
5. Il a peur **de** se faire mal.
6. On hésite **à** réserver nos vacances maintenant.
7. Elles sont sur le point **de** partir.
8. Le directeur tient **à** remercier tous ses employés.
9. N'oublie pas **de** te brosser les dents.
10. Il cherche **à** réussir sans travailler.
11. Elle a accepté **de** m'aider ce samedi.
12. Est-ce que tu continues **à** étudier pendant les vacances ?
13. On vient **de** partir.
14. J'ai réussi **à** arrêter **de** fumer.
15. Tu devrais essayer **de** travailler un peu plus.

CHAPTER 28

1. Aller **au** Koweït
2. Aller **en** Italie
3. Aller **au** Canada
4. Aller **au** Vietnam
5. Aller **en** Irak
6. Aller **en** Égypte
7. Aller **au** Ghana
8. Aller **en** Chine
9. Aller **au** Royaume-Uni
10. Aller **en** Inde
11. Aller **au** Sri Lanka
12. Aller **en** Thaïlande
13. Aller **en** Iran
14. Aller **en** Tanzanie
15. Aller **au** Qatar
16. Aller **en** Espagne
17. Aller **au** Liban
18. Aller **en** Argentine
19. Aller **au** Kenya
20. Aller **au** Pérou
21. Aller **en** Turquie
22. Aller **aux** Philippines
23. Aller **en** Afrique du Sud
24. Aller **au** Nigéria
25. Aller **au** Japon
26. Aller **en** Australie
27. Aller **au** Mexique
28. Aller **en** Colombie
29. Aller **aux** États-Unis
30. Aller **en** Indonésie
31. Aller **au** Brésil
32. Aller **en** Jordanie
33. Aller **en** Malaisie
34. Aller **au** Bangladesh
35. Aller **en** Arabie Saoudite
36. Aller **au** Pakistan
37. Aller **en** Syrie
38. Aller **en** France
39. Aller **en** Allemagne
40. Aller **en** Afghanistan

CHAPTER 29

1. Présent de l'indicatif : Je **fais** du sport tous les jours.
2. Imparfait : Quand on était enfants, on **faisait** toujours du vélo dans la rue.
3. Futur simple : Elle **fera** de son mieux.
4. Subjonctif présent : C'est important que nous **fassions** attention à notre alimentation.
5. Passé composé : Hier, j'**ai fait** du jogging dans le parc.
6. Impératif : **Fais** attention de ne pas te brûler !
7. Conditionnel présent : Si j'avais plus de temps, je **ferais** du bénévolat.
8. Subjonctif présent : Il faut que tu **fasses** des efforts pour réussir.
9. Passé récent : Je **viens de faire** toute la vaisselle.
10. Imparfait : J'ai préparé le dîner pendant que tu **faisais** la sieste.
11. Futur proche : Elle **va faire** plus d'études mais elle ne sait pas encore quoi.

12. Subjonctif présent : Il faut que tu **fasses** ton lit tous les matins.

13. Passé composé : Pourquoi est-ce que tu **as fait** ça ?

14. Conditionnel présent : Il **ferait** n'importe quoi pour recevoir une augmentation.

15. Futur simple : Un jour, je **ferai** le tour du monde.

CHAPTER 30

1. **Est-ce que tu as faim ?**

   Oui, j'ai faim.
   Non, je n'ai pas faim.

2. **Est-ce que tu bois du café le matin ?**

   Oui, je bois du café le matin.
   Non, je ne bois pas <u>de</u> café le matin.

3. **Est-ce que tu es né(e) en janvier ?**

   Oui, je suis né(e) en janvier.
   Non, je ne suis pas né(e) en janvier.

4. **Est-ce que tu as un stylo ?**

   Oui, j'ai un stylo.
   Non, je n'ai pas <u>de</u> stylo.

5. **Est-ce que tu as trouvé mon téléphone ?**

   Oui, j'ai trouvé ton téléphone.
   Non, je n'ai pas trouvé ton téléphone.

6. **Est-ce que tu veux aller prendre un café ?**

   Oui, je veux aller prendre un café.
   Non, je ne veux pas aller prendre <u>de</u> café.

7. **Est-ce que le train est à l'heure ?**

   Oui, le train est à l'heure.
   Non, le train n'est pas à l'heure.

8. **Est-ce que le magasin est ouvert ?**

   Oui, le magasin est ouvert.
   Non, le magasin n'est pas ouvert.

9. **Est-ce que tu fais du sport ?**

   Oui, je fais du sport.
   Non, je ne fais pas <u>de</u> sport.

10. **Est-ce que tu aimes la crème glacée ?**

    Oui, j'aime la crème glacée.
    Non, je n'aime pas la crème glacée.

11. **Est-ce que tu seras là ce soir ?**

    Oui, je serai là ce soir.
    Non, je ne serai pas là ce soir.

12. **Est-ce que tu parles français ?**

    Oui, je parle français.
    Non, je ne parle pas français.

13. **Est-ce que tu es heureux/heureuse ?**

    Oui, je suis heureux/heureuse.
    Non, je ne suis pas heureux/heureuse.

14. **Est-ce que tu sais nager ?**

    Oui, je sais nager.
    Non, je ne sais pas nager.

15. **Est-ce que tu as fini de manger ?**

    Oui, j'ai fini de manger.
    Non, je n'ai pas fini de manger.

CHAPTER 31

1. **Quelle** est ta matière préférée à l'école ?
2. **Quel** est ton plat préféré ?
3. **Quels** sont les pays que tu aimerais visiter ?
4. **Quelles** musiques est-ce que tu as choisies ?
5. **Quelle** est la jupe que tu préfères ?
6. **Quelles** habitudes est-ce que tu essayes de prendre ?
7. **Quels** sont les livres que tu recommandes ?
8. **Quel** est ton film préféré ?

9. **Quelles** langues est-ce que tu parles ?

10. **Quelle** est ton opinion ?

11. **Quel** jour est-ce que tu es libre ?

12. **Quelle** est ta saison préférée ?

13. **Quels** sont tes objectifs ?

14. **Quel** est ton nom ?

15. **Quelles** sont les villes que tu as visitées ?

CHAPTER 32

1. Ce problème est plus **difficile** que je ne le pensais.

2. Il fait **chaud** aujourd'hui. On devrait aller à la plage.

3. J'aime quand la maison est **propre**.

4. Le village où on est restés était **calme**.

5. Il est arrivé **premier** au marathon.

6. Cette blague n'est pas **drôle** du tout.

7. J'étais **ravi** de te voir après autant de temps.

8. Il est toujours **fatigué** après sa journée de travail.

9. Ce pull est vraiment **doux**.

10. Elle est **heureuse** maintenant qu'elle a un **nouveau** contrat.

11. Mon cousin est **timide** depuis qu'il est **petit**

12. Paris est une **grande** ville où il est **facile** de se perdre.

13. Nous étions **tristes** d'apprendre la nouvelle.

14. C'est la **meilleure** glace de la ville.

15. En hiver, il fait souvent **froid** dans cette région.

CHAPTER 33

1. Beau – Quel **beau** manteau !

2. Chaud – J'ai besoin d'une douche **chaude**.

3. Vieux – Mon voisin est un **vieil** homme.

4. Nouveau – Est-ce que tu as reçu ta **nouvelle** carte d'identité ?

5. Libre – Il y a des places **libres** au premier rang.

6. Meilleur – C'est la **meilleure** tarte que j'aie mangée.

7. Troisième – Il a réussi la **troisième** fois qu'il a essayé.

8. Effrayant – Il a lu une histoire **effrayante** aux enfants.

9. Dernier – C'était sa **dernière** journée au travail.
10. Bon – Elle a toujours une **bonne** excuse.
11. Vrai – Ce film est basé sur une histoire **vraie.**
12. Vert – Le pull **vert** te va mieux que le noir.
13. Heureux – C'est un moment **heureux** pour toute la famille.
14. Petit – Elle est toujours avec son **petit** chien.
15. Rouge – Son rêve était d'acheter une voiture **rouge.**

CHAPTER 34

1. La **vieille** maison en pierre va être rénovée.
2. Mes **nouvelles** chaussures sont arrivées ce matin.
3. Ce bâtiment est un **bel** exemple d'architecture.
4. C'est un **nouveau** bouquet de fleurs ?
5. Ses meubles ont l'air **vieux** mais ils sont **nouveaux.**
6. C'est un **bel** endroit pour se promener.
7. Elle porte un **vieux** collier.
8. La maison qu'on a visitée est **belle.**
9. Est-ce que tu as reçu le **nouvel** horaire ?
10. Le **vieil** homme qui habitait ici est décédé.
11. Les **nouveaux** arrivants reçoivent un sac cadeau.
12. Il a un **beau** sourire.
13. Ta **nouvelle** jupe est vraiment **belle.**
14. Pascal est un **vieil** ami.
15. C'est une **belle** histoire d'amour.

CHAPTER 35

1. Qu'est-ce que tu **fais** ce soir ?

    → **Faire** conjugated in the present tense takes the ending **-ais.**

2. La **nouvelle** édition vient juste de sortir.

    → **Édition** is feminine so **nouveau** should be **nouvelle.**

3. Il veut qu'on parle **du** projet avant la réunion.

    → The preposition **de** becomes **du** when followed by a masculine singular noun.

4. Est-ce que tu sais jouer **du** piano ?

→ **Jouer** + **piano** requires the preposition **de**, which becomes **du** before **piano**.

5. Est-ce que tu as eu le temps de préparer le dîner ? Non, je **n'**ai **pas** eu le temps de préparer le dîner.

→ The use of negation (**non**) requires the use of **ne ... pas**.

6. Il a réussi **à** changer ses pneus tout seul.

→ **Réussir** is followed by the preposition **à**.

7. J'ai lu ce **vieil** article hier soir.

→ **Article** is a masculine noun starting with a vowel so the adjective should be **vieil**.

8. Notre voyage **en** Australie était incroyable.

→ **Australie** starts with a vowel so it's preceeded by **en**.

9. J'ai **fait** du café. Est-ce que tu en veux ?

→ The past participle of **faire** is **fait**.

10. **Quelle** glace est-ce que tu veux ?

→ **Glace** is feminine singular so **quelle** should be used.

11. Elle est souvent **pensive**.

→ **Pensif** agrees with the subject, **elle**, so it should be **pensive**.

12. C'est un **beau** tableau que tu as peint.

→ **Tableau** is masculine singular = **beau**

13. J'ai envie **d'**un chocolat chaud pour me réchauffer.

→ **Avoir envie** is always followed by **de**.

14. Pourquoi est-ce que tu refuses **de** leur parler ?

→ The verb **refuser** is followed by the preposition **de**.

15. Est-ce que vous êtes déjà allés **aux** États-Unis ?

→ **États-Unis** is always plural so the preposition before it should be **aux**.

CHAPTER 36

1. ~~français~~ – française – Je pense qu'elle est **française** mais je ne suis pas sûre.
2. ~~certains~~ – certain – Tu es **certain** de ce que tu dis ?
3. ~~seul~~ – seule – Elle est la **seule** à m'avoir répondu.
4. nombreux – ~~nombreuses~~ – Les joueurs sont **nombreux** à participer.
5. ~~heureux~~ – heureuse – Elle est **heureuse** pour la première fois depuis longtemps.
6. social – ~~sociale~~ – Il n'a jamais été très **social**.
7. petits – ~~petites~~ – Ces pneus sont plus **petits** que je ne le pensais.
8. difficile – ~~difficiles~~ – Ce questionnaire est vraiment **difficile**.
9. ~~ouverts~~ – ouvertes – Les portes seront **ouvertes** à 9 heures du matin.
10. déçu – ~~déçue~~ – On espère qu'il n'est pas **déçu** de ses résultats.
11. craintif – ~~craintive~~ – Mon chat est **craintif** depuis qu'il est petit.
12. ~~fou~~ – folle – C'est une idée complètement **folle**.
13. désolé – ~~désolée~~ – Il est **désolé** de t'avoir fait de la peine.
14. créatifs – ~~créatif~~ – Mes enfants sont toujours **créatifs**.
15. ~~précis~~ – précises – Est-ce que ces mesures sont **précises** ?

CHAPTER 37

1. Infinitif : avoir   Présent de l'indicatif : Nous avons
   J'**avais** 25 ans.

2. Infinitif : habiter   Présent de l'indicatif : Nous habitons
   On **habitait** à la campagne.

3. Infinitif : vouloir   Présent de l'indicatif : Nous voulons
   Pourquoi est-ce que tu ne **voulais** pas aller en vacances ?

4. Infinitif : écrire   Présent de l'indicatif : Nous écrivons
   Cet auteur **écrivait** un peu tous les jours.

5. Infinitif : être   Présent de l'indicatif : Nous sommes
   C'**était** une belle journée pour une promenade.

6. Infinitif : porter   Présent de l'indicatif : Nous portons
   Elle **portait** des lunettes pour lire.

7. Infinitif : passer   Présent de l'indicatif : Nous passons
Nous **passions** une agréable journée à la plage.

8. Infinitif : vendre   Présent de l'indicatif : Nous vendons
Ce magasin **vendait** des habits et des chaussures.

9. Infinitif : réserver   Présent de l'indicatif : Nous réservons
Mes parents **réservaient** toujours leurs vacances en dernière minute.

10. Infinitif : boire   Présent de l'indicatif : Nous buvons
Je **buvais** du café tous les matins.

11. Infinitif : faire   Présent de l'indicatif : Nous faisons
Il **faisait** beau.

12. Infinitif : apprendre   Présent de l'indicatif : Nous apprenons
Les élèves **apprenaient** un peu de français quotidiennement.

13. Infinitif : nettoyer   Présent de l'indicatif : Nous nettoyons
On **nettoyait** la maison une fois par semaine.

14. Infinitif : goûter   Présent de l'indicatif : Nous goûtons
Infinitif : cuisiner   Présent de l'indicatif : Nous cuisinons
Elle **goûtait** toujours tout quand elle **cuisinait**.

15. Infinitif : oublier   Présent de l'indicatif : Nous oublions
Il **oubliait** toujours quelque chose à la maison.

CHAPTER 38

1. J'ai mal **à la gorge**.
2. J'ai mal **au ventre / à l'estomac.**
3. J'ai mal **à la tête.**
4. J'ai mal **à l'oreille.**
5. J'ai mal **aux dents.**
6. J'ai mal **aux pieds.**
7. J'ai mal **au doigt.**
8. J'ai mal **à la jambe.**

9. J'ai mal **au poignet.**

10. J'ai mal **au cou.**

CHAPTER 39

1. Regarder – On **regardera** ce film ce week-end.
2. Faire – Ma grand-mère **fera** mon gâteau préféré pour mon anniversaire.
3. Téléphoner – Je **téléphonerai** à mon amie après le travail.
4. Venir – Mes petits-enfants **viendront** me rendre visite bientôt.
5. Chercher – Je **chercherai** un nouveau travail quand j'en aurai besoin.
6. Rendre – Elle te **rendra** ton livre quand elle l'aura fini.
7. Arriver – Le bus **arrivera** aux alentours de 10 heures.
8. Finir – Les enfants **finiront** leurs devoirs avant le dîner.
9. Lire – Je **lirai** ton livre pendant les vacances.
10. Dormir – Nous **dormirons** dans une auberge de jeunesse pendant le voyage.
11. Manger – Je **mangerai** moins de sucre demain.
12. Parler – On **parlera** à notre banquier pour un nouveau crédit.
13. Montrer – Je te **montrerai** comment faire.
14. Voir – Tu **verras**, c'est plus facile que tu ne le penses.
15. Aller – J'**irai** peut-être avec elle au cinéma.

CHAPTER 40

1. Ils **vont avoir** la réponse de l'avocat demain matin. (avoir)
2. Le chanteur **va arriver** à l'hôtel dans quelques heures. (arriver)
3. Demain, je **vais visiter** Rome. (visiter)
4. Elle **va écrire** un livre sur son voyage. (écrire)
5. On **va aller** au cinéma après les cours. (aller)
6. Tu **vas voir** si tu veux venir avec nous. (voir)
7. Est-ce que tu **vas rendre** l'argent à tes parents ? (rendre)
8. Je **vais regarder** dans ma chambre si je trouve ton téléphone. (regarder)
9. Les professeurs **vont préparer** les collations pour la journée. (préparer)
10. On **va être** quelques minutes en retard. (être)
11. Les clients de l'hôtel **vont pouvoir** utiliser la piscine demain. (pouvoir)
12. Il **va falloir** relire les documents avant de les signer. (falloir)
13. Tu **vas prendre** ton sac avec toi ? (prendre)

14. Il **va devoir** accepter les règles de sa nouvelle école. (devoir)
15. Le pianiste **va jouer** son morceau le plus célèbre. (jouer)

CHAPTER 41

1. Courir – Passé composé : Il **a couru** pour attraper le bus mais le bus ne l'a pas attendu.
2. Avoir – Futur simple : Tu **auras** de la chance si tu gagnes le gros lot.
3. Être – Présent : Vous **êtes** toujours les bienvenus.
4. Plaire – Passé composé : Est-ce que ce film t'**a plu** ?
5. Faire – Présent : Nous **faisons** du vélo ensemble quand il fait beau.
6. Prendre – Passé composé : Tu **as pris** des cours de danse quand tu étais petite ?
7. Annoncer – Futur simple : Ils **annonceront** le gagnant après le tirage.
8. Devoir – Imparfait : On **devait** se voir hier mais elle a annulé.
9. Estimer – Passé composé : L'agent immobilier **a estimé** la maison pour la vendre.
10. Falloir – Présent : Il **faut** que tu prennes soin de toi.
11. Pouvoir – Futur simple : Je **pourrai** t'aider avec tes devoirs après le dîner.
12. Aller – Conditionnel présent : J'**irais** au restaurant plus souvent si je pouvais.
13. Prévoir – Passé composé : Tu **as prévu** assez de temps pour étudier ?
14. Rendre – Futur proche : On **va rendre** visite à mes grands-parents ce soir.
15. Venir – Passé composé : Harry **est venu** avec nous au concert.

CHAPTER 42

1. Est-ce que tu as vu ce film ?
   Direct object: **ce film**   Direct object pronoun: **le – l'**

2. On prépare le dîner ensemble.
   Direct object: **le dîner**   Direct object pronoun: **le – l'**

3. Le chat a attrapé la souris.
   Direct object: **la souris**   Direct object pronoun: **la – l'**

4. J'ai perdu mes clés.
   Direct object: **mes clés**   Direct object pronoun: **les**

5. Il a acheté ces fleurs pour sa femme.
   Direct object: **ces fleurs**   Direct object pronoun: **les**

6. Mon chien cherche son os dans le jardin.

Direct object: **son os**   Direct object pronoun: **le – l'**

7. On voit mon frère dans la foule.

Direct object: **mon frère**   Direct object pronoun: **le – l'**

8. J'ai appelé Julie mais elle n'a pas répondu.

Direct object: **Julie**   Direct object pronoun: **la – l'**

9. Nous avons attendu le train mais il a été annulé.

Direct object: **le train**   Direct object pronoun: **le – l'**

10. Elle a adoré ses cadeaux.

Direct object: **ses cadeaux**   Direct object pronoun: **les**

11. On a écouté sa nouvelle chanson.

Direct object: **sa nouvelle chanson**   Direct object pronoun: **la – l'**

12. J'attends Sarah pour aller faire un jogging.

Direct object: **Sarah**   Direct object pronoun: **la – l'**

13. Les élèves écoutent le professeur.

Direct object: **le professeur**   Direct object pronoun: **le – l'**

14. Tu as compris la leçon ?

Direct object: **la leçon**   Direct object pronoun: **la – l'**

15. Elle a commandé sa nouvelle robe.

Direct object: **sa nouvelle robe**   Direct object pronoun: **la – l'**

CHAPTER 43

1. Est-ce que tu as vu **ce film** ?

Est-ce que tu l'as vu ?

2. On prépare **le dîner** ensemble.

On le prépare ensemble.

3. Le chat a attrapé **la souris**.

Le chat l'a attrapée.

4. J'ai perdu **mes clés**.
   Je les ai perdues.

5. Il a acheté **ces fleurs** pour sa femme.
   Il les a achetées pour sa femme.

6. Mon chien cherche **son os** dans le jardin.
   Mon chien le cherche dans le jardin.

7. On voit **mon frère** dans la foule.
   On le voit dans la foule.

8. J'ai appelé **Julie** mais elle n'a pas répondu.
   Je l'ai appelée mais elle n'a pas répondu.

9. Nous avons attendu **le train** mais il a été annulé.
   Nous l'avons attendu mais il a été annulé.

10. Elle a adoré **ses cadeaux**.
    Elle les a adorés.

11. On a écouté **sa nouvelle chanson**.
    On l'a écoutée.

12. J'attends **Sarah** pour aller faire un jogging.
    Je l'attends pour aller faire un jogging.

13. Les élèves écoutent **le professeur**.
    Les élèves l'écoutent.

14. Tu as compris **la leçon** ?
    Tu l'as comprise ?

15. Elle a commandé **sa nouvelle robe**.
    Elle l'a commandée.

CHAPTER 44

1. Il **m'**a acheté un collier quand il était en vacances.
2. Ce costume **te** va très bien.
3. Est-ce que je peux **vous** demander quelque chose ?
4. Il **nous** a dit qu'il allait vendre sa maison.
5. Est-ce que tu **lui** as écrit cette année ?
6. On **leur** a envoyé leurs cadeaux d'anniversaire.
7. Il **nous** a répondu hier soir.
8. Fais attention, tu vas **lui** faire mal.
9. J'espère qu'il va **me** pardonner.
10. Est-ce qu'il **vous** a parlé de son nouveau projet ?
11. Je **te** promets de venir à ton spectacle.
12. Il **leur** a raconté une histoire avant de dormir.
13. Plus tu grandis, plus tu **lui** ressembles.
14. Le vétérinaire **m'**a téléphoné pour **me** rappeler l'opération de mon chien.
15. Ce n'est pas moi qui **lui** ai volé son argent.

CHAPTER 45

1. Est-ce que tu es déjà allé **à Disneyland** ?
   Est-ce que tu **y** es déjà allé ?

2. On a décidé de ne pas aller **au cinéma** ce soir.
   On a décidé de ne pas **y** aller ce soir.

3. Est-ce que vous avez besoin **d'argent** ?
   Est-ce que vous **en** avez besoin ?

4. Je vais **à la boulangerie** sur le chemin du travail.
   J'**y** vais sur le chemin du travail.

5. Il travaille **au centre-ville**.
   Il **y** travaille.

6. Tu bois **du café** ?
   Tu **en** bois ?

7. J'ai acheté un bouquet de fleurs **au marché**.

   J'**y** ai acheté un bouquet de fleurs.

8. Il y a **de l'eau** dans son bol.

   Il y **en** a dans son bol.

9. Tu as pris le train pour aller **à Lisbonne** ?

   Tu as pris le train pour **y** aller ?

10. On mange **des pommes de terre** plusieurs fois par semaine.

    On **en** mange plusieurs fois par semaine.

11. Est-ce que tu es sûr **de cette réponse** ?

    Est-ce que tu **en** es sûr ?

12. Tu vas **à la plage** demain matin ?

    Tu **y** vas demain matin ?

13. Qu'est-ce que tu penses **de mon pull** ?

    Qu'est-ce que tu **en** penses ?

14. Elles habitent **dans cet appartement** depuis quelques années.

    Elles **y** habitent depuis quelques années.

15. Elle a hérité **de cette maison**.

    Elle **en** a hérité.

CHAPTER 46

1. Tu veux venir avec **nous** au cinéma ?
2. Ce colis vient d'arriver. Je pense que c'est pour **vous.**
3. Elle est toujours fière de **moi**.
4. Tu te souviens d'**eux** ?
5. Mon frère est aussi grand que **toi**.
6. **Eux**, ils ne me parlent jamais.
7. Tyler et **lui** sont amis depuis qu'ils sont petits.
8. C'est **toi** qui viens de m'appeler ?
9. **Lui,** je ne l'aime pas beaucoup.

10. Ce portefeuille est à **moi**.

11. Elle vient cet après-midi pour passer du temps avec **nous**.

12. J'ai eu de meilleures notes qu'**elles**.

13. On l'a attendue mais on est partis sans **elle**.

14. **Moi**, je n'ai pas envie d'y aller.

15. Est-ce que ce livre est à **toi** ou à **lui ?**

CHAPTER 47

1. Mon ami **qui** sera là ce soir, vient de perdre son travail.

2. Elle a adoré le cadeau **que** tu lui as acheté.

3. C'est toi **qui** m'as appelé ?

4. **Qui** est là ?

5. J'ai trouvé la boucle d'oreille **que** j'avais perdue.

6. Le film **qu'**on a regardé hier soir n'était pas terrible.

7. Tu connais déjà mes amis **qui** seront à la fête.

8. C'est ce **que** j'ai dit.

9. On a réservé une place dans le train **qui** part à deux heures.

10. Voilà le document **que** tu m'as demandé.

11. Le chien **qui** aboie est le chien des voisins.

12. J'ai finalement trouvé les clés **que** j'avais perdues.

13. On est allés au restaurant **que** tu nous as recommandé.

14. Tu entends les oiseaux **qui** chantent ?

15. C'est elle **qui** est toujours en retard, pas moi.

CHAPTER 48

1. **travailler** – Il faut que nous **travaillions** moins.

2. **nourrir** – Il faut que tu **nourrisses** le bébé.

3. **acheter** – Il faut qu'elle **achète** ses billets d'avion avant qu'ils soient trop chers.

4. **attendre** – Il faut que j'**attende** mon mari pour partir.

5. **tondre** – Il faut qu'il **tonde** la pelouse.

6. **ranger** – Il faut que je **range** ma chambre.

7. **agir** – Il faut qu'on **agisse** au plus vite.

8. **trouver** – Il faut que tu **trouves** une solution.

9. **réussir** – Il faut que vous **réussissiez** vos examens.

10. **économiser** – Il faut que nous **économisions** plus.

11. **étudier** – Il faut que j'**étudie** pour mes examens.

12. **arrêter** – Il faut qu'ils **arrêtent** de fumer.

13. **marcher** – Il faut que tu **marches** plus vite.

14. **parler** – Il faut qu'elle **parle** à son patron de son idée.

15. **vendre** – Il faut que je **vende** cette maison.

CHAPTER 49

1. Je lis un article **intéressant** dans le journal.

2. Elle perd ses écouteurs deux **fois** par jour.

3. Le mari **de** ma tante est mon oncle.

4. Ma **grande** sœur est née en janvier.

5. Ce chien est **tellement** adorable !

6. J'ai **honte** de mes résultats.

7. N'oublie pas de te brosser les dents **après**.

8. Ma grand-mère a de plus en plus de cheveux **blancs**.

9. Il ne porte **jamais** son alliance.

10. C'est facile pour toi de dire **ça**.

11. Ce film est beaucoup **trop** long !

12. On a acheté nos **nouveaux** bijoux à la bijouterie.

13. Mes voisins ont adopté un **petit** garçon.

14. Je prends **toujours** une douche le soir.

15. Ce plat est trop **salé** pour moi.

CHAPTER 50

1. ~~un~~ – **une** – Je viens de voir **une** étoile filante.

2. **clous** – ~~cloux~~ – Sa boîte de **clous** est tombée de l'étagère.

3. ~~architect~~ – **architecte** – L'**architecte** a approuvé les plans finaux.

4. **espagnole** – ~~espagnol~~ – Ma femme est **espagnole**.

5. ~~était~~ – **sera** – On **sera** au marché ce samedi pour vendre nos légumes.

6. ~~Ils~~ – **Elles** – Ce sont Julie et Laura. **Elles** sont cousines.

7. **le** – ~~la~~ – J'ai mis **le** journal sur la table pour toi.

8. ~~s'habille~~ – **m'habille** – Je **m'habille** toujours après mon petit déjeuner.

9. **réveille** – ~~se réveille~~ – Elle **réveille** les enfants tous les jours à 7 heures.

10. ~~sa~~ – **la** – Il se rase **la** moustache une ou deux fois par semaine.

11. **cette** – ~~ce~~ – Est-ce que tu as vu **cette** promotion ?

12. **aurais** – ~~aurai~~ – J'**aurais** plus de temps pour moi si je travaillais moins.

13. **avoir** – ~~être~~ – Tu ne devrais pas **avoir** honte de ton travail.

14. ~~ma~~ – **mon** – J'ai pris **mon** anorak mais je l'ai laissé dans la voiture.

15. **ces** – ~~ses~~ – Tu sais à qui sont **ces** chaussures ?

16. **leur** – ~~leurs~~ – **Leur** idée était bonne mais pas géniale.

17. ~~Vingt-et-un~~ – **Vingt et un** – **Vingt et un** joueurs participent à la compétition.

18. **a** – ~~est~~ – Il **a** descendu le tableau au garage.

19. ~~été~~ – **eu** – J'ai **eu** beaucoup de chance quand j'ai acheté ma maison.

20. **étudier** – ~~étudié~~ – Il a toujours besoin de calme pour **étudier**.

21. ~~à la~~ – **au** – Demande **au** caissier de te donner un sac en papier.

22. **du** – ~~de~~ – Je me souviens **du** vieux bâtiment qui a été détruit.

23. **à** – **de** – Tu as tort **de** ne pas faire attention à ton argent.

24. ~~au~~ – **en** – On sera **en** Grèce à la fin de la semaine.

25. **apprennes** – ~~apprends~~ – Il faut que tu **apprennes** ta leçon.

26. ~~Quel~~ – **Quelle** – **Quelle** est ta série préférée ?

27. ~~faux~~ – **fausses** – Je pense que ces réponses sont **fausses**.

28. **vieil** – ~~vieux~~ – Le **vieil** ascenseur de notre immeuble est toujours en panne.

29. **superstitieux** – ~~superstitieuse~~ – Est-ce qu'il est **superstitieux** ?

30. **était** – ~~étaient~~ – On **était** proches avant de vivre dans différentes villes.

31. ~~à la~~ – **au** – Je ne sais pas ce que j'ai fait mais j'ai mal **au** poignet.

32. **feras** – ~~ferais~~ – Tu **feras** la lessive quand tu rentres ?

33. **vient** – ~~a~~ – Elle **vient** de recevoir son diplôme.

34. ~~tu~~ – **toi** – Cet appartement est parfait pour **toi** !

35. ~~qui~~ – **que** – Ce n'est pas la chanson **que** j'ai entendue.

THANK YOU

Thank you for choosing the *French Grammar Workbook* as your language learning companion. I sincerely hope that it helped you improve your French skills and that you have enjoyed exploring the most common French Grammar and Conjugation rules.

My goal with this book was to provide a comprehensive review of the most common rules and plenty of extra practices and activities for French learners. As always, I would greatly appreciate your feedback, so please consider leaving a review where you purchased this workbook.

I always create content for French learners, either on my YouTube channel, Instagram, or website. You can find all my resources and links at www.theperfectfrench.com.

I hope you found this workbook helpful in your language-learning journey.

Once again, thank you for choosing the *French Grammar Workbook*. I wish you all the best in your progress toward becoming more fluent in French every day!

Dylane

MY BOOKS

The Complete French Courses – Including books, videos, and audio.

> **The Complete French Pronunciation Course**
> **The Complete French Conjugation Course**
> **The Complete French Grammar Course**
> **The Complete French Vocabulary Course**
> **The Complete French Expressions Course**

Conjugation Textbooks – Including books, video, and audio.

> **Passé Composé vs Imparfait**
> **The French Subjunctive**

The French Short Stories – Including books and audio.

> **French Short Stories – Volume 1**
> **French Short Stories – Volume 2**
> **French Long Stories – Volume 3**

My Free Self-Study Guide – Including all my lessons listed and my study plan.

> **The Complete French Self-Study Guide**

Download my free self-study guide at **www.theperfectfrench.com/freebies**.